THE HIGH ROAD

Memories from a Long Trip

THE HIGH ROAD

Memories from a Long Trip

Mark Herndon

Fresh Ink Group
Roanoke

THE HIGH ROAD
Memories from a Long Trip

Fresh Ink Group
An Imprint of:
The Fresh Ink Group, LLC
PO Box 525
Roanoke, TX 76262
Email: info@FreshInkGroup.com
www.FreshInkGroup.com

Edition 1.0   2016

Edited by Stephen Geez

Book design by Ann Stewart

Cover design by Jason Perkins

Cataloging-in-Publication Recommendations/BISAC Subject Headings:
BIO004000 BIOGRAPHY & AUTOBIOGRAPHY / Composers & Musicians
BIO005000 BIOGRAPHY & AUTOBIOGRAPHY /
Entertainment & Performing Arts
MUS010000 MUSIC / Genres & Styles / Country & Bluegrass

Library of Congress Control Number: 2016934172

ISBN-13: 978-1-936442-23-2

Dedication

To everyone chasing a dream:

Never forget that the journey can be
the best part of getting there.

"Departing the Fix Outbound"

A term used in navigation to describe the point at which a vessel, aircraft, or person has passed over a specific point in space or time and is now proceeding on to the next waypoint or destination.

Table of Contents

Foreword

Several months before my father passed away in 1998, I asked him to write some memoirs for me. I wanted his take on a life that spanned almost 80 years across some incredible times in American history. I thought his untold "Greatest Generation" tales from fighting in combat, sailing the seven seas, flying at the edge of space as a test pilot, and putting boots on the ground in some of the world's darkest corners would make priceless reading someday for both my daughter and me.

A man of few words, he simply said, "Nah, couldn't tell it like it really was." I pestered him as much as I dared a few more times until he finally said, "Nope. That's mine, son. Maybe you should start writing yours instead." I thought about it for a while and began to realize exactly what he meant by telling it like it really was. It's daunting. Unless the audience has been there and seen the elephant themselves, they can only relate topically. I respected him all the more for keeping mum. I put the idea away for sixteen years. It was always something I could do later.

Reminiscing with a friend one night, I was encouraged to start writing down some of the tales I was telling. As I get older, I realize later might mean never. Memory often fails to serve at an alarming rate. Thinking of my daughter and remembering how badly I wish my dad had put his stories to paper, I thought I would start typing out some yarns from the old days just for my kid to have as a keepsake. *Maybe she might know her dad a little better someday. Maybe she might find some things here to help reference where she comes from. Maybe through hindsight, I could spare her the pain of consequence from not listening to the voice of true self, which sometimes is just a whisper in a room full of shouting.* One story led to another, then another, and soon I had enough to start a manuscript.

I started with growing up in the often-tumultuous world of a military family's nomadic existence, and with how the desire to belong to something almost led me down the road to ruin. My fortuitous change of path after that was the roundabout reason I eventually realized many dreams—and also woke up to many realities—while spending most of my life on the road under the vaunted, but often unfriendly, spotlight of celebrity.

I have made my living as both a musician and a pilot. This co-vocation is not all that unusual. I've known many who love the same two mistresses. In my flying career, sometimes I flew passengers who, in the music world, were celebrities. Surprisingly, while immersed in my music career, as well, I knew a number of them who shared my dual passion.

The spirited conversations resulting from some of those encounters revealed this to me:

We are addicts of a different kind, willing to put ourselves through more than the average hardship and disappointment just to get the fix of channeling our spirit to a crowd of people, or of soaring free above the Earth—the fix from a drug that produces the ultimate high, the *high* of fulfillment and, sometimes, long after the party's over, the ultimate *low* of irrelevance.

In the pages to come, I'm going to try to capture the way things were for nearly thirty years on the road with the band. Of course, just like my dad, there are some stories from the edge of space and dark corners of the world that I will never tell. I, too, have seen the elephant more than once. Where necessary, I may have forgotten a few details, so I reckon this work could be classified as a tell-*almost*. For me, as I hope it is for you, it is one wild, joyful, terrifying, educating, and ultimately sobering ride.

Welcome. Get comfortable in the recliner.

There's a seatbelt if you need it.

Oh! I have slipped the surly bonds of Earth
And danced the skies on laughter-silvered wings;
Sunward I've climbed, and joined the tumbling mirth
Of sun-split clouds—and done a hundred things
You have not dreamed of—wheeled and soared and swung
High in the sunlit silence. Hov'ring there,
I've chased the shouting wind along, and flung
My eager craft through footless halls of air. . . .

Up, up the long, delirious, burning blue
I've topped the windswept heights with easy grace
Where never lark, or even eagle flew—
And, while with silent, lifting mind I've trod
The high un-trespassed sanctity of space
Put out my hand, and touched the face of God.

"High Flight"
John Gillespie Magee, Jr.
August 1941

CHAPTER 1

Murphy's Law

Cruising through the sub-stratosphere at over 400 knots, I *thought* I could fly anything with wings. With about a thousand hours of flying time under my belt at the time, I figured I had seen it all. Something happens to flyers around that milestone in the logbook that tends to embolden us in certain ways. Sometimes, those ways get a few of us killed.

When you start flying as a teenager, as I did, that 1,000-hour number seems almost light years away. When you get there, you allow yourself the luxury of thinking yourself special to have made it this far, and you have a tendency to think you're credible. That's laughable now because, in reality, that's the level at which a person really starts learning to fly. But you can't tell that to a cocky twenty-something, ten-foot-tall rock star who was burning jet fuel every day. Up to this point, I was ready to take on Chuck Yeager.

I was the drummer for one of the hottest-selling, highest-grossing bands of all time—a band that took the name of a proud Southern state and made it a household name around the world. The wild decade of the 1980s was drawing to a close and we were riding the apex of success, with the last couple of years finding us, at last, flying high above the tedium of road travel by bus. Like many enveloped in the purity of high altitude, I experienced everything—sounds . . . sights . . . life—as if it all had a sharper edge.

5 June 1988

It was a beautiful day, sparkling clear and unseasonably cool for this time of year. We had just finished an afternoon outdoor show near Augusta, Maine, at a sold-out venue. The band was *on*, and the crowd kept bringing us back for encore after encore.

It was the last show before heading home for a much-needed break after about a month of non-stop touring. Needless to say, everyone was feeling good that afternoon as we loaded our bags, food, and spirits onto the plane for the ride home—no spirits for me just yet, for obvious reasons.

"Conquest twelve, oh eight Alpher, maintain flight level two ninah zeero, contact Washington Centah, one tree tree point two five—so laaahng." The voice with a curt, New England accent crackled in my headset as the Boston air-traffic controller (ATC) handed us off to the next sector down the line in Washington.

I keyed the mic, repeated the numbers back to him with an added farewell of my own, and spun the frequency into the radio. I made the call to Washington; they took us aboard and I sat back and took in the view—just normal inflight routine stuff. The lazy afternoon progressed to evening as beautiful Maine receded in the distance. With a rather unusual tailwind in our favor, the countryside of Pennsylvania slipped by far below at seven miles a minute. Typically, it is the other way around in that direction, and hardly *ever* a tailwind if you're going *home* from *anywhere*. But, fortune had smiled, and I wasn't about to question it.

To my right, the sun began its dive for the horizon, bathing the cockpit with a gorgeous soft-orange light; the deep royal blue of high-altitude sky above my head created an amazing contrast. I could see all the way down the coast toward our nation's capital, the Potomac River disappearing beneath a light cloud cover as it wound its way into the Chesapeake Bay.

Craning my neck back over the left wing, I could make out the skyline of Philadelphia off to the north with the Atlantic Ocean vanishing toward Europe. The towering black maw of night's darkness rose up over the eastern horizon, enormous, foreboding, and coming for us. The air was smooth as glass. Looking down, I could see the ground becoming dark. Lights came on in the towns, and curving bands of white and red outlined the roads that looked like illuminated fiber optic cables darting in various directions—traffic. At this altitude, nearly six miles up, it was still daylight; the curvature of the Earth provided for this phenomenon. *Ah, life is good.*

Aviators have a saying for these magical moments—fat, dumb, and happy. It's a cynical way of saying, "This is wonderful, but the shit's probably gonna hit the fan any moment." We just sort of laugh at it—Murphy's Law—gallows humor. It's part of the job.

There were two of us in the cockpit. My friend—my first mentor in flying—Larry Ashbrook sat in the left seat as Captain. I sat as First Officer in the right.

When the band purchased an airplane to ease the grind of more than 330 days a year on a bus, Larry came with it. He had been a test pilot for Cessna on the then-revolutionary Conquest 2. It could fly faster and higher than any other propjet on the market in those days.

ATC guys used to question our altitude and ground speed when we would check on frequency in the mid-30s flight levels. Once in a while, I'd hear a smart-aleck remark from the airline jocks about a turbo-prop invading their pure jet altitudes. I loved it. I was very proud of that airplane and proud to fly it.

Larry had flown the Conquest from the first prototypes out of the factory through all the initial design flaws and fixes. He had more time in that bird than anyone in the country and knew it better than anyone, so it was logical—and a windfall for the band—that he got the gig.

Oddly, he and I didn't like each other right off the bat, probably because we were really a lot alike, at least in a lot of ways we would discover later.

With a few flights together under our belts, and having shared a few experiences on the road, we started to build a friendship. Larry was the life of the party kind of guy, not the picture you might conjure of a typical corporate pilot. He was hardcore motorcycle all the way. Back before it was the norm for every banker to have a hog in his garage, Larry was a dedicated biker, a hell-raiser without equal who never took any shit from anybody. He was the smoothest talker with the ladies I have ever known. He was a real character.

Man, we used to get some looks at the terminals—me with my long hair, shades, and holey jeans; and Larry with his bushy beard, Harley t-shirt, tattered shorts, and flip-flops. In comparison to all the other business-attired pilots standing around the FBOs (Fixed Based Operator or general-aviation terminal), we probably looked pretty disgusting. We thought it was hilarious. It probably wasn't. Those were the days.

In the air, though, Larry was nothing but serious, as was I. No halo shimmered above my head, for sure, but I always took the flying part of my life very seriously, and I loved the learning curve I was on. Larry had just the right amount of confidence and caution; he knew when to push the envelope and he knew when to hold back. He always had my back, too, when I was about to screw up. I thought he would have made a great squadron skipper in the military fighter-jet world. I would have flown into combat with him any day.

"Well, Herndon, less than an hour until wing party," Larry said over the headset.

The Loran Navigation computer was showing fifty-eight minutes until landing in Fort Payne, Alabama, our home field. We kept a fridge stocked with beer in the hangar for all the homecomings. In case the fridge was empty, we always somehow remembered to grab a case out of catering to put in the baggage compartment where it would keep super cold for later.

When we parked and shut down, the married guys would all head home. After the plane was put away and the paperwork done, Larry, one or two of the staff guys, and I would sit around and have a few beers to debrief from our escapades. It got to be a tradition. That hangar still stands today, and I am very glad the walls are silent.

"Yeah, man, ready for a cold one," I said. And I was. The thrill of that afternoon's show was still coursing through my veins and I was ready to celebrate. Thank goodness we were almost home. It was nothing but smooth sailing from here on out.

Beep! Beep! Beep! "Warning! Warning!" sounded in my headset. Directly in front of me appeared a one-inch square, a very bright flashing red light. Flashing red lights are never good, certainly not at 31,000 feet; and most certainly not a light that reads Master Warning. It's bright and says that for a reason. Your headset beeps and screams "Warning!" for a reason. That's to get the attention of fat, dumb, and happy pilots immediately. I snapped out of my daydream quicker than a scalded cat. By the time I could say, "Aw hell," Larry was already on it.

When you get a Master Warning, the first thing you do is check the annunciator panel to see what the fuss is all about. Usually, it's something relatively minor that can be fixed or dealt with en route. You accomplish the memory items for that particular event, follow up with the published checklist, and go along your merry way. Usually . . .

"Battery overheat," Larry said calmly. I looked at the temp gauge. It was rising!

Back in those days, turbine-powered aircraft mostly used NiCad batteries. They had more voltage for engine starts than your good-old-fashioned lead acid car-type batteries. The trouble was, when they died, they died fast—no gradual decay like car batteries. To remedy this problem, other than buying a new one every year—which wasn't very cost effective—the solution was to send the battery off to the manufacturer and have it deep cycled. It's a rather complicated procedure, so I'll just call it a rebuild, basically. Your battery comes back good as new, for half the cost, and it's good-to-go for another year or so.

We kept a record of engine starts in order to stay ahead of the life curve for this particular battery. We knew it had been deep cycled only about two months prior, so what the hell could be the matter with it?

Well, something was; after we had unloaded some of the electrical system's pull on the battery and checked the generators for malfunction, the core temp was still rising.

Now we had a real problem on our hands. Upon reaching a certain temperature due to overheat, NiCad batteries can and will go into what they call thermal runaway, a nasty little trait. Nothing you do to ease the draw on the battery, not even shutting it off, will stop the rise in temperature until—you guessed it—it explodes into a fireball.

In this case, the fire would have been spread out over several miles on the ground—remnants of burning debris from an airplane blown to bits in the sky. Nice mental picture—a pretty good remedy for constipation when you're strapped to that airplane if you allow that picture to develop. We now had a race against the clock.

The guys with the lab coats and slide rules had done battery-overhead tests on the ground when companies started putting NiCads on the market for aviation. They would torture them until they either burned or blew, then scurry away like squirrels, writing numbers in their little books. They scurried away because the explosion was something like a quarter stick of dynamite. Each battery was different as far as how long it took to catch fire to blow up, so they averaged out a timeline from the start of thermal runaway to the Big Bang.

If I remember correctly, all the *POH* (*Pilot's Operating Handbook*) said about a battery overheat was, "A temperature increase above 164 degrees can result in battery components uncontrollably rising in temperature and igniting with possible explosion of battery core. Evacuate aircraft immediately." *Brilliant. Yep, that's a good idea. Open the door and get out. The first step is only six miles straight down. Now we have a problem, and now we really don't know if we are going to make it.*

When people work together as a team—whether playing ball, playing music, or flying an airplane—it's a beautiful thing. In aviation, it is rhythmical and precise. Crew coordination is drummed into your head relentlessly. It has to be, because when there is an emergency, especially a pressing one, only training will keep panic at bay. Specific tasks are to be performed at certain times by both pilots, respective to what seat you are in. The left seat basically flies the aircraft; the right seat handles all the radio and nav, and performs the items on the appropriate checklist.

Anytime we used to fly dead head legs, which are flights with no one on board, we would practice hypothetical emergency procedures. Strangely, only about a week before, we had done this for an emergency-descent scenario, so it was fresh in my head.

"Declare an emergency, Mark," Larry said. I could see concern on his face, but he remained calm. At least he appeared to. Another friend of mine taught me some wisdom about interpreting the FAA regulations that state: "In order to act as pilot in command of an aircraft, a person must . . . blah, blah, blah." The key word here was "act."

I pressed the mic button. "Washington Center, Conquest one two zero eight Alpha, declaring an emergency." I hoped I sounded calm, too. I doubt it, though—this was my first real emergency. The controller came back immediately and said, "Zero eight Alpha, roger, describe nature."

He wasn't asking my opinion about the sunset at this point; he wanted to know what was wrong so they could begin the process of clearing the airspace of other traffic below us, contact the airport tower where we intended to land, roll the fire trucks, etc. I gave him a brief picture of the problem while dialing the international distress code, 7600, into the flight identification transponder.

While Larry clicked off the autopilot, pulled the power levers back to flight idle, I pushed the prop condition levers up into flat pitch. This bleeds off airspeed quickly so you can drop the landing gear and extend the first notch of flaps out at the required airspeed. As the airspeed indicator passed through 200 knots, slowing rapidly, I reached over and dropped the gear, selected the first notch, and dialed the field elevation into the cabin pressurization system.

Larry rolled us into a sixty-degree bank to the left as the nose came down through the horizon. The reason for the bank is to use centrifugal force to keep unfastened passengers in their seats. If you just simply push the nose over at these speeds, people who are not in their seatbelts and items not fastened will float weightlessly all over the cabin—and those people won't be very happy.

With the descent established, we rolled the wings level with twenty-five degrees nose down showing in the AI (attitude indicator). Now, twenty-five degrees nose down doesn't sound like much, but in this type of aircraft, it felt more like eighty degrees.

As we bid farewell to the high altitude twilight and descended into darkness, it felt like the unseen Earth was rushing up at us. The rate of descent indicator was pegged at 6000 feet-per-minute. By pegged, I mean that's all the system could show, so there's no telling how fast we were coming down. It was probably closer to eight or ten thousand feet per minute. That equates to around 80 to 100 miles an hour, straight down. Just like the book said, though, the airspeed was right on the money at 180 knots because of all the drag from the gear, flaps, and flat pitch props.

"Advise the cabin, EMER descent checklist," Larry commanded, fully absorbed in flying the descent as precisely as possible. I advised, told everybody to buckle up, and said we'd be on the ground very soon. I was met with blank stares from some ashen faces. I understood. It's worse back there when you don't really know what's going on. Again, that's the beauty of crew coordination. One guy flies while the other does the busy work, which is so much more efficient and safer than a single pilot trying to manage everything.

Memory items completed . . . I worked the checklist silently. When I finished, I simply said, "EMER descent complete." There's no time for extra chitchat at times like this. I could hear the ATC guy working his butt off down below, clearing away all the other flights.

We were headed to Dulles Airport because, fortunately, it was nearby and had the best emergency ground equipment—like fire trucks and ambulances. *Ah-ah! No, don't let your mind go there! We got to get this thing on the ground. We can worry later!*

Despite the cold fear in my gut of the ticking time bomb sitting right in front of my feet, I remember thinking how awesome the whole system was—to enable just one aircraft to literally own the airspace all around a busy airport like Dulles, even at rush-hour, once an emergency is declared.

As we descended through FL240 (twenty-four thousand feet), we were switched to a low altitude controller who was already advised of our condition. I heard a few "Good luck, fellas" on the radio from some of the airline guys on the same frequency. *Cool! A little "brotherhood" shot in the arm.* It's funny what goes through your mind at the oddest moments.

"I'm off," I said to Larry. No, I wasn't going on a union break, I was notifying him that I was switching over to the other radio in order to get the latest Dulles weather and that I'd be right back.

The current conditions near the surface had suddenly taken a turn for the worse. True enough, it had been clear as a bell all day along the Eastern seaboard, but I guess after the sun went down, things must have cooled rapidly. It was overcast now at eight-hundred feet, with light rain, visibility two miles, wind out of the Northwest at twelve gusting to eighteen—no big deal under normal operating conditions, but now we had to fly the published IAP (instrument approach procedure). That would have been no biggie, either, but as I said earlier, it was now a race against the clock. Had it been clear, we could have saved precious minutes going directly to the airport visually.

With a solid cloud deck below, there was no choice but to fly the IAP. That cold feeling in my gut just got a little colder. *Oh well, got a job to do. No time for that crap.* I dialed the navigation radios to the published frequencies, entered in corresponding altitude and go-around information, and briefed Larry on the crucial parts of the approach.

I punched the mic button again. "Dulles. Runway one right. Top three thousand, inbound zero one one, set twice. Intercept nineteen hundred, down to five hundred twelve, which is two hundred above, radat (radar altimeter) set two hundred. Missed is climb to eight hundred, then climb right to three K, heading zero six zero. I'll give you progressive. We are cleared for the approach, and localizer coming alive."

Sounds like gibberish, but it only takes a second to relay volumes of information if you know the language. It's standard procedure and really handy in a pinch.

Larry banked left to intercept the localizer and line us up on the runway we still could not see.

We talked briefly about evacuation. I figured the guys in the back, knowing them, would have the door open and be out of there as soon as we came to a stop, if not before. Everyone had also been taught how to use the exit window.

I reached down between my knees and unclipped one of the locks holding the fire extinguisher in place. We would be the last out, and if we caught fire on the ground, I was going to be ready to fight my way out quick.

The controller handed us off to the tower and they cleared us to land.

About a half mile from the outer marker beacon, Larry gave the order for full flaps. I pulled the handle and we started down the final descent, still in the clouds, me still holding my breath. We had gotten this far, though, and my confidence was beginning to build that we might just beat the clock after all . . .

But, you never count hound dogs before they come out from under the porch.

Just below eight-hundred feet, we broke out of the overcast and could see through the rain. Runway One Right was lit up like a Christmas tree. It was way more beautiful than the sunset we had left upstairs. For added decoration, all kinds of lights from emergency vehicles flashed on either side of the runway. They were there for us.

They, too, were prepared for the worst.

That got my attention right back to business. I looked everything over and said, "Final check complete" to let Larry know everything was done that needed to be done and all he had to do was land.

I called out airspeed and descent rate—

And the old boy greased the landing!

I was almost a little jealous.

That airplane was fantastic at flying in and out of short fields, which we did a lot—not that Dulles has short runways. Runway One Right is two and a quarter miles long, but that plane had the ability to land at about 105 knots and stop on a dime.

With full reverse pitch on the props and heavy braking, you could have that baby at a standstill in less than fifteen hundred feet if you were sharp. Well, old Larry was pretty sharp, so the fire trucks didn't have to chase us long at all. We stopped right there on the runway, spitting distance from the big numbers on the approach end. The emergency trucks came up all around the plane.

Just as I predicted, the guys in the back were out the door within seconds after we shut the engines down, headed at a brisk trot for the grass at the side of the runway.

The shutdown checklist took only seconds and was all a memory by this time. I grabbed the fire extinguisher and climbed out of the seat with Larry right behind me, shouting, "Go! Go! Go!" *Hell, what was his problem? I was moving at light speed at this point.* The fear of burning to death is quite a motivator.

Once outside, I went forward to see if the moon-suited firefighters needed help locating the battery compartment. Of course, they didn't. They already knew where it was, so they yelled at me to get the hell away.

I joined the others at the side of the runway and watched as the firefighters bravely removed the bomb from the nose of the bird. By now there was smoke coming out of the baggage compartment where it was located. They took it about a hundred yards up the runway and off the pavement where a foam truck proceeded to smother it with fire-retardant foam. Another foam truck was guarding the plane in case that smoke turned to fire . . . and a good thing—we had some important stuff in there: cold beer!

Some of the aluminum flooring in the baggage compartment melted; when they cut it open, the firefighters guessed the battery had around two more minutes before explosion. They also discovered that it had never been deep cycled. The FAA and NTSB would later come down hard on the company that confirmed this had been done—and rightfully so.

You hear about these stories where, in tight spots, people recount things slowing down, as though they were watching a slow-motion replay of everything that happened in the moment. I don't remember any of that. I do remember that after the initial shock of realizing we had a serious problem in the air and the potential for unpleasant death came and went, everything came into very sharp focus, lucidity and a situational awareness like I never had before.

I could see everything that needed to be done, in my mind in perfect order, almost from an outside-the-body perspective. I wasn't worried, and somewhere way in back of my mind, I knew we were going to make it. The end of everything was not going to happen on that day. We weren't going to let it win—neither of us.

Wherever that dimension is in our brains, I can tell you, it compartmentalizes fear and turns you on—I mean really *on*. You kind of surprise yourself at how calm and efficient you are processing megabytes of information, while your body just follows commands. It's not that I have any desire to fly broken airplanes, but it is a real high and kind of hard to describe.

Or maybe I'm just nuts.

The guys flew home the next day on the airlines. Larry and I stayed in DC with the plane. That night, we earned ourselves one hell of a hangover for the next day. We got back down to business the second day and saw to it a new battery was installed and the aluminum flooring in the baggage compartment was repaired.

We flew the plane home to Fort Payne about four days later, just in time to pick everyone up again for another five weeks out on the road.

It was truly life in the ultra-fast lane. The events of that early June day, in the sky over Dulles International, eventually faded into a distant memory.

There would more harrowing things to come.

A footnote . . .

Larry left about five years after the Dulles incident; he headed to Eastern Airlines to fly Boeing 727s.

A particular memory I have of those days flying with him is late one moonless night on the way toward the next stop on the tour. We were flying across the Gulf of Mexico, the shorter route being a straight line between Ft Myers and Panama City, Florida.

It took us out over open water, far from the sight of land-based lights. The Milky Way formed a luminescent canopy above our heads while the space below, where the Earth should have been, was nothing but a black void.

Everyone in the back was sound asleep. The clock on the panel was nudging 3 a.m. It was a beautiful night, and old Murphy wasn't going to bother us this time.

If it had not have been for the singsong drone of the props just outside the window, pulling us forward, I would have thought we were just hanging motionless somewhere in deep space.

Looking up through that thin, clear air of high altitude, the stars and planets seemed within an arm's reach. I felt privileged to behold such a beautiful sight, a vision that makes one realize just how lucky he is to be a pilot, and then how small he really is in the midst of God's unfathomable creation.

We turned the cockpit lights down to get a better view, and sat in silence for a while.

He suddenly shivered almost convulsively.

I looked at him and asked, "What's the matter, man? Somebody walk across your grave?"

He was quiet for a minute, then said, "Nah, I just know I'm gonna die on that bike someday; it will never be in an airplane."

Scoffing at him, I said, "Aw hell, Larry, you'll live forever with your Irish luck and that medal around your neck."

He just shook his head, and we continued on in silence.

His mother had given him a Saint Christopher's medallion when he first started flying as a kid like me. He always wore it around his neck.

Not long after he got the Eastern Airlines gig as a 727 first officer, he departed the fix outbound.

He got run off the road by a drunk driver near Lexington, South Carolina, in front of a Catholic church, on a road called "The Devil's Backbone." He hit a tree and died on his Harley.

How strange are life's ironies. For some unknown reason, Larry wasn't wearing his medallion that night. His mom wanted me to have it, but I just couldn't take it from her.

Prayers, blue skies, and tailwinds for you, my friend, wherever you are. I hope you're at the biggest, wildest bike rally ever.

CHAPTER 2

Cat Shots and Gypsy Blood

"Why is America lucky enough to have such men?
They leave this tiny ship and fly against the enemy.
Then they must seek the ship, lost somewhere on the sea.
And when they find it, they must land upon its pitching deck.
Where did we get such men?"

From *The Bridges at Toko-Ri*
James A. Michener

*   *   *

There's a race of men that don't fit in,
A race that can't stay still;
So they break the hearts of kith and kin,
And they roam the world at will.
They range the field and they rove the flood,
And they climb the mountain's crest;
Theirs is the curse of the gypsy blood,
And they don't know how to rest.

Robert W. Service

*   *   *

I stared up at the models dangling in formation, hung by fishing line from the ceiling of my bedroom, engaged in dogfights, dive bombing or formation flying, and I wondered how many kids, like me, knew what they wanted to be when they grew up. I always knew I would fly someday.

"Dinner is served!" My mom's usual call to supper came floating down the hall from the kitchen. I washed up and joined my father at the table.

"What's the latest addition to the fleet?" Dad asked, referring to my crowded ceiling.

"The F-4 Phantom," I said, hoping to stir some conversation with a guy who flew one.

"Mmmm." He spoke volumes with this one sound. Just based on inflection,

I always knew what was being conveyed.

After my mother sat with us, I silently dove into the meal. My mom came from a rather aristocratic background. Her father had risen to become president of Sealtest Dairy Company. Her family lived in a well-to-do section of Springfield, Massachusetts, although my grandfather would eventually die broke.

My mom and dad lived with her parents for a brief stint soon after they were married, before Dad shipped out to war in the Pacific. "Tough looking, but well-dressed men," Dad would tell me, "with names like *Vinnie Da Hat* and *Joey No-Nose* would come to the house at all hours of the night, demanding to see your grandfather. He had a little problem down at the horse track."

I don't know how bad it got, but I do know that when he died before I was born, my grandmother had no choice but to sell their house to help pay off the debt. She wound up with nothing.

The first time I ever walked into a casino, I remember my gut doing flip-flops. My conscience was screaming, "Get out!" Ignoring that completely, I placed a twenty-dollar bet on the roulette wheel. The guy snatched the money out of my hand, put it in the slot, and spun the wheel again. I lost the bet, of course, and seeing my money disappear in the blink of an eye made me sick.

To this day, I don't play. Nothing against it, really. I'm just not interested. It bores me to death. Maybe it's the spirit of my grandfather, who paid such a high price in losing the game—and his life because of it—that kicks me in the gut.

My grandmother was a concert pianist with the New York Philharmonic Orchestra for a while, and Mother was an accomplished musician in her own right. Classical music rang from the piano in our house. The two of them would play for hours.

As a young woman, my mother saw the footlights on the stage of Broadway; she starred as Eliza, the lead in *My Fair Lady,* which ran for a year just before World War II broke out. She later attended Endicott College just outside of Boston, where she met my father.

An odd couple at first, I would imagine—a sophisticated city girl with a budding acting career on the horizon—and a tall, dark, handsome, rough-cut farm boy with brand new shiny gold Naval Aviator wings on his chest. "It was irresistible love at first sight," she would often tell me.

Mom departed the Broadway lights for a hard, unglamorous life as a military wife; adjusting to long separations and tough, lean years as she and my dad drove back and forth across the country, moving from base to base before I was born.

The only way to travel back then was via the famous Route 66. I can't imagine what that must have been like for them—the now legendary Americana unfolding in front of them for days on end as they pressed onward. Maybe it wasn't so tough . . . pretty romantic, if you ask me.

I think we were a smaller, more bonded country back then—Norman Rockwell's country. I imagine every town they passed through likely provided an experience different from the last. By the time I would crisscross that same country hundreds of times both by land and air over a quarter-century later, it would be far more homogenized.

Franchises and superhighways would eventually make travel easier in many ways, but it seemed to me that I somehow missed out on something: the slower pace of travel then, allowing time for the rush of unbridled freedom to soak in; total immersion in the sensuality of wide open, unpopulated spaces; actually having time to meet and chat with people along the way; and the thrill of seeing snow-capped Rockies for the first time, abruptly jutting up from the endless, undulating, prairie sea.

I visualized my parents weary, dusty, but young and happy, arriving in a small West Coast town called Los Angeles—just your basic mid-sized American town with no freeways, freaks, or smog. Places like San Diego and Malibu were little hick towns just a day's drive away.

Oh, and there was this odd little hamlet up in the hills called Hollywood where movie stars lived.

Elegance, not debauchery, was *de rigueur*. From listening to my mother's stories, I sensed a stronger bond of civility back then between people from the eastern shore of Maryland all the way to the scintillating waters of the California coast.

There are still short stretches of miles here and there, sections that have been preserved in places where a lingering remnant of the old Route 66 spirit can be found. You have to really stop and listen, pause, and imagine those days, an era when exceptionalism, self-reliance, determination, and a united people overcame the odds, and PC were just two letters in the alphabet.

Every once in a while in my travels, I came across a few mom-and-pop motels, restaurants, and campgrounds still sporting the motif and décor of those grand days, but they were usually located across the street from a Walmart or some national hotel chain you can find anywhere. Now, you leave for a road trip, drive for five days, and what do you find? The same shops, eateries, and motels you left at home.

My dad was a career Marine fighter pilot for thirty-five years. As I grew up, he was somewhat aloof around me. At age twelve, I sensed an air of authority that I feared greatly. He was tall, lean, and a hell of a hard ass. He was a man's man and a Marine all the way. If you've ever seen the movie *The Great Santini* starring Robert Duvall, you've met my dad. He was very much like that fictional character, Wilbur "Bull" Meechum, except more stoic.

His stoicism frustrated me a bit at times—like at the dinner table where I hoped to engage him in maybe talking about the F-4 model I was working on.

Dad had seen combat in World War II, Korea, and again in Vietnam; but he never talked about it around Mom or me. He never told war stories at all, but some of the exploits that my mom shared with me validated his steely image.

I finished my meal quickly and asked to be excused.

"What's the rush?" Dad asked.

"Still a few hours of daylight," I explained. "Gonna ride down to the river for a little bit."

As I headed out the front door, I heard my father say to no one in particular, "Mmm . . . restless kid."

Mother shrugged and said, "Gypsy blood."

I hopped on my bike and headed for the docks. I grew up on Marine air stations around the country; I enjoyed moving from base to base. I looked at it as an adventure, and it cultivated my excitement to look forward to the next port. Jets constantly screamed overhead, coming back from who knows where.

I will never forget the unmistakable sound of the F8U Crusader busting into the pattern, right at the speed of sound, with the oil-cooler doors open to make even *more* noise.

WHHOOOM! BOOM! I can still hear the signature moaning of the F-4 Phantom on approach to landing, the pilot constantly jockeying his throttles for the right sink rate.

WheeeEEEU! WheeeEEEU! WheeeeeEEE! The distinctive snarl of the A-4 Skyhawk, or throaty roar of the A-6 Intruder at full power on takeoff, clawing its way toward the sun.

Lying in my bed at night, I loved the sound of the old-fashioned radial-powered Grumman S-2 Tracker rumbling down the runway a mile or so away. I would listen as it gathered enough speed to finally break gravity's hold and become airborne, the engines' deep growl changing to a lower pitch and fading off as it climbed away.

I knew them all just by sound without ever having to look. You just can't help it once it's in your blood.

After a few minutes of furious pedaling through the neighborhood, I reached the riverbank where most of my friends were waiting. "C'mon, man! Where ya been?" one hollered as I crested the small rise.

Below me lay the aircraft carrier. Her deck was covered with parked aircraft, their tail sections perched precariously over the water, waiting for their turn to be launched. On the flight deck, men and machines scurried, readying to catapult the next jet off the bow of the ship to slice through the tropical waters of The South China Sea . . . *my* jet.

To an unitiated adult, this "ship" was just a flimsy boat dock that jutted about fifty feet out into the brackish dark waters of the Neuse River. Sometimes adults don't get to see things as clearly as kids. At the front of the ship a ramp constructed of two-by-sixes pointed up and out over the open water beyond.

Like me, all of the guys were into planes—fighter planes, mostly. We watched in awe from the schoolyard and neighborhood, wondering whose dad was in the jet at the moment. We were all caught up with it.

Since my dad never shared stories at home, it created a kind of mystique that drove me to want to be like him and his fellow pilots—the ones he hung out with down at the flight line or the officer's club, garbed in flight suits and swagger.

Besides all of the replicas hanging in flight from our bedroom ceilings, we were seriously into flying the gas-powered model planes controlled by a handle with two strings on it, going around and around, wide open. Two of us would get in the middle of the circle and dogfight our models till we either got so dizzy from turning in circles that we couldn't stand up any longer, or until one would ram the other's craft, sending both to the ground in a spectacular crash. Undaunted, we'd either figure out how to fix the damaged airframes or build more. We "flew" our bikes everywhere. Riding around the neighborhood, we were on a mission, flying formation on one another's wing or dogfighting again.

But, this evening's event was my favorite—cat shots—and I was dead serious about this. We'd ride hell bent for leather down from the crest of the hill, onto the dock, and up the ramp, falling at last into the water, bike and all.

"You're up, Herndon," one of my friends said.

I grinned. They didn't need to twist my arm.

I pushed my bike back up the hill and mounted it. I stared down at the aircraft carrier, now looking a bit narrow from where I was poised. I thrust the bike forward and peddled with all my might. The tires hit the wooden planks with a whir. Off the end and out into space I went.

My heart soared!

That brief moment of airtime in the sky . . . flying high the above the sea . . .
Delirious!

Bike and rider hit the water, which was about eight feet deep. I let the bike sink to the bottom. They threw me a rope. I swam down and tied it to the bike. I climbed out of the water as they pulled up my bike and got it ready for another's turn.

Daylight waned as the fun progressed. My fourth run, however, resulted in pilot error. Just before rocketing down the dock, I lost control and crashed. My friends laughed hysterically.

"Hey, dickhead!" one of them yelled. "Where'd you learn to fly?"

I lay there for a moment, motionless, bracing for the tidal wave of pain. The laughter died down.

"Hey, man, are you okay?" another asked.

I sat up, trying to figure that out for myself. I was scraped up pretty good, and my neck and shoulder hurt like hell. They helped me up and I limped home.

As I walked into the house, my mom and dad took notice of the blood and my left shoulder, which was now at an odd angle.

"What happened?" my mom asked.

I shrugged. "I had a wreck. My shoulder hurts." Mother grabbed her purse and car keys. "C'mon, we better go to sick bay and have a look at that."

Dad barely looked up at all. "It happens," he muttered wryly. I could only imagine what he was referring to with the pitching deck of a *real* aircraft carrier.

I didn't get into any trouble, nor did I get much sympathy.

Mom drove me to the clinic and we were assigned a room to wait for the doctor. "I'm sorry," I said as we waited.

"It's okay, dear," she said, staring out the window for a moment. "I'm glad you weren't hurt badly, but I'm afraid the course for many bumps and bruises in your life has been charted."

"Whaddya mean?"

She smiled wistfully and, still looking out the window, began. "Your father and I were married for thirteen years before you came along. Early on in our marriage, a doctor had informed me that I would never have kids. I was very sad, but life goes on. Then, in 1953, I came down with a case of typhoid fever."

I watched as my mom reached back in time. In those days, typhoid fever was a death sentence. The disease killed people by the scores. Medicine was not very advanced, not even close to what it is now. Antibiotics were still brand new, and the doctors really didn't know what to do.

She was one hell of a fighter, though, and she fought like a lioness for her life. She lived past the date the doctors predicted. She was literally on her death-bed when she began a miraculous turnaround. "I needed a blood transfusion very badly," she continued, "but I have a rare blood type. The hospital didn't have any units of blood that matched. One of the other pilots' wives put out a call to the squadron, asking for anyone with this blood type to donate, if they could. It turned out, one of the enlisted guys of Eastern European descent had my blood type. I think his family was from Romania or somewhere in that region."

She paused briefly as an orderly came for her signature on some paperwork. "In true Marine fashion, he stepped up to the plate and donated as much as he could over several days and weeks, knowing that at the rate I needed blood, his health was at risk, too.

It saved my life.

I started to recuperate and, after several months, was back to health. I had been sick for almost a year." She sighed, remembering just how sick she had been, then squeezed my hand.

I knew it was a tough year for her. During this time, my dad, just home from Korea, would still be deployed off and on. They only saw one another every now and then. It must have been unbelievably hard. People just don't realize the stress and sacrifice military families and marriages endure.

"Anyway," she added, "after I got well, and against the odds, I became pregnant with you. So it must have been that gypsy blood, that same blood from the Romanian guy, that saved me." She smiled at me, her eyes moist. "You know, they say people who have it in their veins tend to have a *thirst* for life—a life on the edge—a thirst for adventure and wanderlust that carries them throughout life. Maybe this *thirst* makes up a part of *you*, Mark."

She suddenly became stern. "Don't *ever* settle for anything or anyone that ties your spirit to the ground, or you will *die* from that thirst for life not being quenched."

My mother always had a way with words. I remember listening to that story and thinking something special was going to happen to me someday.

The doctor finally came in and checked me out. It turned out that I had broken my clavicle. There's not much you can do for a broken clavicle except just grin and bear it. I had to take it easy for a while, but it didn't take long before I was at it again. I guess by today's standards, all of us boys would have been put on some kind of behavior-management medicine, but back then it just seemed normal to be out and about, doing something.

With a wink, my mother would always say it was the blood from the transfusion that changed things, allowing her to have such a restless son. I don't question it; moms have a way of knowing.

Oddly, from my earliest memories on, I have always been the happiest—and most at peace—in motion, moving or going somewhere. I still am. I have had the wanderlust all my life.

Maybe the Gypsy blood thing isn't so farfetched after all.

CHAPTER 3

New Kid in Town

"Don't worry about being the new kid here; everybody is pretty cool" said Glenn, who was one of the first—and few—kids at public school to become my friend.

It was a scary and confusing time; things had changed in my idyllic young life in 1968 when dad went to Vietnam. All of my friends' dads got orders about the same time. Our fathers would be gone fifteen months. My little group of *Stand by Me* friends and I went our separate ways. The families had to leave on-base housing to move across the country to wait for the men to come home from war. Some of them wouldn't.

In March of 1968, I watched my dad fly off into the great unknown. I remember that day well—the jets taxiing away from the crowd of families that stood on the flight line. One by one, they would pull forward and turn away from us, heading towards the waiting runway. The hot jet wash and smell of kerosene bathed us in the stark reality of how serious a thing these men were embarking on. It is a strange, almost exhilarating, feeling to witness this tradition. Mixed emotions filled me as I watched my father and other dads, husbands, brothers, and sons go off to war.

I could see his white helmet in the cockpit. He looked our way for only a second, dark visor and oxygen mask obscuring his face as he nudged his Phantom forward and turned away towards the runway. He was focused on the job, already compartmentalized. I would learn this skill years later as a means of compartmentalizing the pain of leaving my own family so many times. On takeoff, the jets roared by two at a time, breaking ground, pointing their noses at the dull, grey overcast. They vanished into it banking west, leaving only a trail of brown smoke and receding thunder to mark the spot where we would last see them for over a year.

Driving away from the ceremony, my mother put her hand on mine and said, "It's okay, son. You don't have to be the man of the house right now." I cried like a baby even though I had just turned 13. The tears flowed from fear as well as enormous pride. Like my father would tell me years later, "It's hard to explain unless you've been there."

We moved into a small ranch house in Beaufort, North Carolina. It was a great location right on Taylor's Creek and, as the crow flies, only about three or four miles from the open sea. It was part of the Intracoastal Waterway that slices its way from Maine to Florida, providing sheltered transportation to vessels not suited for open-ocean travel.

My dad had given me a little Montgomery Ward ten-foot aluminum skiff with a Sears four-horse motor for my birthday before he left that year. I was thrilled. Although it wouldn't do much more than eight or ten knots wide open, it offered me adventures and a sense of freedom and independence I had not known until then.

My ship and I plied the waters around Beaufort and Morehead City, North Carolina, for many days on end. That small boat, along with a sparse group of friends I managed to make, provided a sort of Huck Finn existence for us in the summers of 1968-69. I say *sparse* number of friends because after moving off base, there was no longer the spirit of all for one, one for all. I enjoyed the camaraderie amongst us military kids; up until now, I naïvely thought that was how it was everywhere.

I befriended a local kid at school named Glenn. He was the first non-military-brat friend I had. I was thirteen now and meeting kids in school who came from all walks of life. In Beaufort, most came from families that scraped a living out of fishing, factory work, or government civilian jobs twenty-five miles up the road at Cherry Point. It was tough for many families to make ends meet, to say the least. A few kids befriended me because I had that little boat, but most shunned me because of the false notion that my parents were rich.

Ha! In my opinion, military pay, then and now, is absolutely atrocious for what the soldiers, sailors, Marines, Coast Guardsmen, airmen, and their families go through to defend this country. The government should be ashamed of doling out only pennies on the dollar as compensation to America's defenders.

Being thrust out of my on-base shelter of like-minded buddies back at Cherry Point and into the real world, I had a lot of catching up to do. The late '60s were a very troubled time in America. The anti-war movement was at a crescendo around college campuses nationwide. It was public poison on the news every night, glorifying the protesters and demonizing the soldiers. This emotional powder keg was beginning to smolder at the junior-high public school level as well.

With my father gone to Vietnam, putting his life on the line every day, I just didn't get it. At thirteen, I couldn't understand why the kids who wore peace signs seemed to hate me because of what my dad was doing. Looking back, maybe they didn't understand things, either; they were just going along with what was perceived to be cool at the time.

Not cool was how much they relentlessly ganged up and picked on me. This was new. I was always very small for my age, with light-blond hair—tow-headed, as they called it—fair-skinned, not good at sports, and I had to wear glasses: a geek. This naturally made me a target of opportunity for the bullies. It infuriated me how the ones who wore the damn peace signs were the meanest.

"Come on," Glenn said. "We better get to class." We walked back into the school building and to the next class, which was Algebra. The bell rang, but the teacher hadn't made it to class yet. I was sitting at my desk in the back of the classroom when a little clique of guys who ran together ganged up on me. Three held me while the other two or three took turns punching and kicking me. As I struggled to free myself, I couldn't believe what I saw. There, amongst the group of bullies attacking me, was *Glenn*. I learned an important lesson that day about some people's real intentions when pretending to be your friend. Of course, my dumb ass had taken the bait. One of the punches from another kid knocked my glasses off. With the others still holding me, Glenn picked them up off the floor, went to the chalkboard, and coated them with chalk dust. He then made a great ceremony of gently placing them back on my face so I could see better.

"There ya go, four eyes. That ought to help," he said. Everybody howled. Those holding me thought, since I couldn't see because of the chalk dust, that it would be funny to watch me try to find my seat, so they let me loose.

Big mistake.

Up until now, I will admit being intimidated by most of the bigger boys. I knew they could hurt me.

The betrayal of someone I thought to be my friend pushed me into a blind, white-hot rage. Fear—of anyone or anything—left me. I took off the glasses, picked up the teacher's wooden pointer, and with a swing that would have made Babe Ruth proud connected with the side of the little two-faced bastard's head. He started to back up in shock, and I jumped on him like a rabid dog. I really started to hurt him, and he went down hard, which surprised me, because I didn't really know how to fight. I sat astride him, beating him in the face for all I was worth.

He started crying and that just made me even madder; I felt like I should be the one crying for what he did to me. I got up and picked up an empty desk, lifted it up over my shoulders, and threw it down on him. While I was screaming something at him, I remember the other tough guys backed away. This was another revelation and another thing I hate about bullies: they don't even have the balls to help one of their own when they're in trouble.

"Knock it off, knock it off!" a loud voice shouted. It was the teacher, a pretty good-sized guy in his own right. In the middle of all the chaos, I found myself immobilized in a painful arm lock. The teacher gripped me with all his strength, perhaps assuming I had started the altercation, dragging me off to the principal's office.

After I sat outside the principal's office for what seemed like an eternity, the teacher came out, gave me a disapproving look, and headed back to his classroom.

The principal came to his door and growled, "Get your ass in here."

"Yes, sir," I said. This was in the days when school kids had to respect authority rather than expect to be pampered by it. To say that I got a royal ass chewing would be an understatement of grand proportion, but the actual ass *whipping* I thought was coming never did. The principal was a retired Marine. He had retired out of Cherry Point. When he finished yelling at me, and his face returned to a shade somewhat less than crimson, he walked me to the door, put his arm around my shoulder, and said, "I think I would have done the same thing, son, and by the way, I bet your dad would be proud of you today. Now get the hell out of my office; I don't want to hear about any more trouble with you involved in it."

Like I said before, things were different back then. The guy I won the fight with that day had to go to the hospital for concussion and a bunch of stitches. I am not proud by any means of hurting him as badly as I did. It did, however, teach me a valuable lesson about bullies. They are chicken shit cowards underneath all the big talk and victimization of someone they think is weaker.

That lesson would serve me well many years later in a life-or death struggle against the same sort of thing, only with a lot more at stake than just teenage pride.

CHAPTER 4

The Free Musketeers

My father returned from Vietnam in early 1970. He got orders back to Cherry Point. It was the new-kid-in-school routine all over again when we moved back from Beaufort. I thought I was going to have to face a whole new set of bullies.

Then the strangest thing happened. Almost all my friends, the guys I'd had so much fun with before we moved off base, they all came back to Cherry Point at nearly the same time. Their dads had gotten the same orders. This is *very* unusual for a military brat. Having friends like I did before Vietnam wrenched everybody away, then seeing them again, just never happens. I guess that's why kids who grow up the way we did make close friends fast. You knew you wouldn't have them for long.

I bumped into two old friends, Karl and Steve, not two weeks after moving back. They were sitting in Steve's driveway as I flew my bike by, going nowhere in particular.

"What the . . . ?" I couldn't believe it. I also couldn't believe how much they both had grown and how much I hadn't. *Oh well*, I thought, *at least it will be like old times and maybe I won't get picked on so much.* Karl and Steve were almost six feet tall.

Later, Ricky and James, two more of our original group of fearless bike pilots, would also move back on base. It was sad to learn about Davey and Jimmy, as they would never get to live on any base anywhere again . . .

Their dads' names are on a black marble wall in Washington, D.C.

I was making friends outside the little group, and two of those were Frankie and Howard.

"I never tried this before," I said one day to Howard.

Frankie stood quietly.

"Aw, we can do it, man," Howard said. "It will be easy if we just plan it."

So right there, the three of us went to work hatching an elaborate plan to skip school for a day. It was early September. None of us, especially me, wanted to go back to the grind. We crafted our mission plan down to the tiniest detail. It involved getting on the bus, getting off the bus, and meeting up at a rendezvous point. From there we would sail five miles across open water on the huge Neuse River. On the other side lay our wondrous destination—an all-girls' camp. We had heard many mysterious things about it from older guys who could drive, and that transfixed our curious young imaginations. We got a telescope and tried to look across to get a glimpse of the goddess-like creatures we knew inhabited the place. Naturally, and soon, we had to execute our plan and go see for ourselves.

Howard was from California, and a year older. He was cool. In those days, anything or anybody from California was seen as really cool. I listened intently to his stories of surfing, sailing, and conquests on the beach when he lived out there. Frankie and I assumed he was an expert at sailing. We also assumed he was full of it on the conquests, but he could tell a good story anyway.

"We can use my sabot," Howard said.

"What are we gonna do?" I asked. "Row all the way across?"

A sabot is a device for changing the bore on a firearm. In this case, though, according to him it was a very small sailboat, about six or eight feet long. Normally used to row from a much larger boat to the dock, it has a detachable mast for a sail. Most people call it a dinghy, but Howard called it a sabot and Howard knew everything about sailing because he was from California. The problem for now, however, was that we had no mast. No sail.

"We can build one," he said, like it was no big deal.

So, we did. Or thought we did, anyway. I stole a bed sheet from my mom's linens. We scrounged up some one-by-fours and a thick dowel rod. We put it together in Howard's garage and took it out for a sea trial that weekend.

It worked pretty well. The sail caught the light breeze, and we moved along at a pretty good clip. Howard turned the rig on the dowel rod and really impressed me, tacking back to shore. We went out about a hundred yards and came back. Yep. We were ready for the seven seas.

The big morning of our plan arrived. "I'm worried about Frankie," Howard whispered as we got on the bus. "Well, if he chokes, we'll just go without him," I said. Frankie was a little high strung and although the same age as I, he was even smaller. We thought he might chicken out from being scared. I felt like we were about to pull off a bank heist. It *was* scary, but thrilling. I was hooked. Mischief. There's nothing like it . . . until you get caught.

The school bus was a rickety old clunker. The back door had no emergency horn the way they do now. A few bus stops later, I walked up to the driver for the first step in the plan—the distraction. "I need to get off here now!" I said to the driver with my best *I'm dying* look on my face. I hopped off the bus and acted like I was getting sick, while Howard and Frankie slipped out the back door. I looked back at the driver. "I have to go back and get my homework.' My mom can drive me, so you go ahead." Back then, they allowed high-school kids with drivers' licenses to drive the bus, so it worked like a charm. Either he had no clue what we were doing or he didn't care. Probably the latter.

We met up and hurried down to the riverbank where we had hidden Howard's boat. We climbed onboard and pushed off with two oars.

As we got farther out into the water, we realized it wasn't a great day for sailing, especially not in an eight-foot boat. The wind was strong and very cold as it gusted across the water. The waves were increasing in size and our makeshift sail was trying to blow away.

"I can't hold it much longer!" I yelled.

The stiff breeze had turned into a gale. Frankie was really scared. "Man, we're gonna drown!" he yelled over the wind.

We were moving at a good rate with the wind generously filling the sail, pushing the tiny boat across the frothy water fast enough to cut a pretty good wake. The far shore of the new world came into clear view, and I started to think we might have a chance.

That thought whooshed away with the sail as it tore itself loose from the mast. I grabbed for it, but too late. It whipped away, twisting and turning in the wind like some airborne worm. We were four miles from where we had launched this tiny rowboat, on open water with four-foot waves coming at us—the foam blowing off the tops of the whitecaps. We were soaked and it was bitterly cold. We realized we had forgotten life jackets.

I wished I had chickened out and stayed on the damn bus!

"All we can do is row with the waves," Howard said. "It's sort of like surfing."

After about a half-mile of earnest rowing, the wind and waves lessened a bit closer to shore. We let them just carry us to the beach. We hauled ourselves up on the bank, shivering in our sodden clothes. I just lay there, hoping the early morning sunshine would warm me up.

"We're in trouble," I said out loud, staring back across to where we had come from.

"No shit, Sherlock," replied Frankie.

"Well, it's not all bad," I heard Howard say from the top of the bank. He was standing there, hands on his hips, just grinning. "Looky here," he said.

I climbed up the slope and . . .

"Holy crap!" I said breathlessly. There was the girls' camp. Somewhere out on the big water I had forgotten about it while being tossed around like a cork going over Niagara, trying to stay upright and survive. The wind had miraculously pushed us right to our destination.

"Let's go see what we came to see," Howard said with a sly grin.

"How we gonna get back in time?" Frankie asked, obviously worried.

Howard snapped, "We'll think of something, and quit worrying every minute!"

With renewed vigor, we strode to the top. Even this far away from home and in another county, we still had the notion we'd be caught skipping school, so we approached the camp with utmost stealth. A wall surrounded the treasures within, so we sneaked, tree-by-tree, up to it.

"Boost me up," I said to Howard.

He made a step out of his hands and lifted me up to peer over the wall. I could hardly wait. I was imagining beautiful girls all running around in various states of clothing, all laughing and playing, and how they would be in total awe of the pirates who had just landed on their shore. With a grin on my face, I puffed out my chest. We were conquistadors! Oh, how I was wrong. There was nothing. Nobody. Not a sound. The place was deserted.

"This doesn't make sense," I said. "There's nobody here."

"Whaddya mean, there's nobody there?" Frankie asked.

"Just what I said. Nobody."

In disbelief, we walked down the length of the wall to where it turned a corner, revealing a chain-linked gate, locked shut. We stood there just staring at the empty grounds, boarded up huts, and parking lot filled only with gravel. Wind-born leaves merrily chasing each other on the breeze seemed to somehow mock us. "Na, na, na-na, na . . . you silly boys. No one here, no one near."

That's when the obvious dawned on us. With a collective "Oooooohhhh shhiiitttt," we realized that the exotic sights we had risked our stupid hides to come and see were all gone because, *duh*, the girls were back in school, too. That's proof positive that the teenage mind, especially that of the male, is not capable of thought processes much above those of a cow.

The task of hitchhiking twenty miles north to Vanceboro, North Carolina, walking back across the drawbridge at New Bern, and panhandling money off the streets for a bus ticket down to Cherry Point was a long and tedious one. Of course, we were caught and served out our harsh sentences. I got what I thought was life without parole. I received some deserved razor strops across my backside, too.

The very drawbridge section, part of the long bridge we walked back across to New Bern, some two decades later would be sold and moved down the Intra-coastal Waterway to be installed at a crossing in North Myrtle Beach, South Carolina. That crossing would be right beside the Alabama Theater, a venue where I would spend a lot of time later in life.

Life's ironies again.

I can definitely understand the importance of teaching a kid about not breaking rules, but at the same time I vaguely remember a sort of twinkle in my father's eyes when he was carving a chunk out of my backside for worrying my mom so much.

No telling how many times as a boy he probably did many a similar thing.

CHAPTER 5

Key Bored

I remember our house, no matter where we lived, always being filled with the sound Mom playing the piano. Mozart, Chopin, and Beethoven would come to life on the ivories as she would play for hours . . . and I always enjoyed the sound of it filling the rooms.

One day, after observing how easily rhythm came to me while tapping some pencils, my mother said, "I think you should take some piano lessons."

I wasn't too keen on it because I was still into building my gas model planes and flying them after school, as well as getting into mischief with my friends. But I figured, what the heck. "Okay," I said. "I'll give it a try." She and my grandmother were so enthusiastic about it I didn't want to let them down.

Mom found a teacher up the road in New Bern, North Carolina. I kept it a secret from the other boys because it was sort of sissy for a boy to be playing piano in those days.

The day arrived for my first lesson. I would take two lessons per week. My mom dropped me off at the teacher's house and drove away. It was frightening. It resembled the house on *The Addams Family* TV show—tall, lurking, a sort of frowning kind of place. The front entrance was covered in overgrown shrubs and vines, and the grass around the home was knee high to a giraffe. It looked as though no one had inhabited the place for years. Big, unkempt, shabby, and foreboding would be an understatement when describing this house. As I dawdled, dragging my feet towards the front entrance, I felt it glaring at me. The shades were all drawn.

I swallowed hard and knocked on the door, and after what seemed like an hour, a huge, bearded bear of a man came to the door and let me in. He was a Russian immigrant from Leningrad. His name was Igor, and he growled rather than spoke. "You are late," he snarled as the heavy door swung shut, hinges creaking eerily.

It was dark as a tomb inside, smelling of musty old books, cat urine, and mothballs. It offered no foyer or living room inside, only pathways throughout the house, established by floor-to-ceiling mountains of sheet music, books, and junk. The guy was a hoarder long before the show came around. Stuff was piled everywhere. The pathways for navigating to necessary parts of the house were defined by the finish worn off the wood flooring and six-foot walls of stuff towering everywhere, like a maze.

He led me to a room towards the back of the house just off the kitchen. It, too, was full, with was just enough room for a grand piano with one dim lamp sitting on top. It was the only illumination in the room. I felt like I was in a time warp.

This has got to be a bad dream. I'm in 19th century London. I've been lured into a torture chamber, I thought to myself.

He sat down next to me on the bench and opened Book One. "Young mahn, you vill be sthaa-tink heeere today, no?" he grumbled in a thick Russian accent.

I said, "No," thinking I was just agreeing with him. He started swearing in Russian, and I hoped that meant the lesson was over. I did get through the lesson and somehow, over the next couple of months, I miraculously managed to make it through Book Two, even though I was terrified of the guy. He would rap my knuckles with a ruler every time I messed up.

I mentioned cat-urine earlier. There must have been thirty cats that lived with him in that spooky, creepy house. They were slinking around everywhere. One or two would even drape themselves across the piano, regarding me with cold, dead eyes, lifeless orbs that would squint and seem to say, "Ahhh! Another one! Heh heh heh. He will cut you into little pieces, and soon we will have you in our dinner!"

To this day, I really can't hit a note on the ivories, though I can't imagine why. I did manage to make it to one recital, however. I had gotten somewhat used to the ruler across the knuckles and didn't want to disappoint my mom and grandmother. It was held for all the parents of his students. The others were all way more talented and advanced than I. Naturally, being at the lowest level of accomplishment compared to the other students, none of whom I knew, I was on the schedule as first to play. I was the opening act, and I was terrified.

There must have been forty or fifty parents and their friends out there for the concert. With my heart not really into it, I was intimidated by some of the other students who could really play. I remember thinking, *What the hell am I doing here? I don't belong here!* I was also scared by the thought in the back of my mind that there might be a really big ruler waiting for my knuckles later on if I messed up.

I had to play three songs from Book Two. I got through the first one okay. I flubbed the second and had to start over. I remember hitting those wrong notes and feeling as though the world was coming to an end, all those people out there just shaking their heads and saying, "What a pity; some kids should just stay away from music."

Now, with my heart in my chest churning out paralyzing fear, I fought my way through the last number. I finished, stood up, and took a quick spastic bow that probably looked more like a convulsion. I beat an even hastier retreat to the sanctuary of the stage wings that fortunately were draped with thick curtains. There I hid with the agony of utterly blowing my performance.

Strangely, I didn't get the ruler afterward.

While I hid behind the curtain, I felt a big beefy hand on my shoulder. I looked up and it was *Ivan the Terrible*— and he was actually smiling at me. "Yoo did well. Yoo trrrie haad goot, no?"

This time I said, "Yes."

In hindsight, it probably wasn't all that bad, but it sure seemed that way. I learned much later in life how much of a perfectionist all musicians really are. We hear things very differently than does the audience. What sometimes seems like a train wreck to us largely goes unnoticed to the listener. I eventually learned that a live audience hears a great performance with their eyes, for the most part. Stage presence, passion, and spastic bows go a long way sometimes. But, that was a long way down the road at this point.

My mother didn't push piano anymore after that. She could tell and, I think, empathize with how much I hated it. She understood in the way fellow musicians do, even though I didn't feel any fellowship then, to say the least. I wanted out forever.

It was the end of piano lessons, *thank God*. Perhaps I should've stuck with it. Maybe it would have made me a better drummer and songwriter later on. Still, you don't think about those things when you're that young. All I wanted to do was get up in the morning and jump into the sky.

Meanwhile, one of my running buddies had a paper route delivering the Raleigh-based *News & Observer*. His father had received orders to another base and had to move away. He asked me if I was interested in taking over the paper route, delivering papers in the mornings before school.

My meager allowance from my folks—if I did my chores—was just not covering what I needed to keep building model planes and buying the gas and supplies for such a hobby. "Sure," I said, "How much do you make?"

He said, "I clear anywhere from forty to sixty bucks a week." In 1971, that was a large amount money for a fourteen-year-old to have in his pocket. So, excitedly, I took the idea to my dad, who subsidized my entrepreneurial spirit with the purchase of a front basket mounted on the handlebars of my bike, along with two saddlebag baskets to be mounted on the rear behind the seat.

I learned the route and got up by 4 a.m. every morning to load papers onto my bike. I got really good at nailing peoples' front doorsteps on the fly. Of course, I was pretending the papers were ordnance to put on target from my aircraft. The arc of the paper at a certain speed probably has a complex geometric formula to land it on a designated spot, but I couldn't tell you any of that. However, I could hit that target every time, despite the weather and whatever watchdog charged in hot pursuit. That formula, or whatever it was, also nailed a lot of road signs and mailboxes by beer bottle later on. Those early mornings, some of them beautiful, were what my dad always called "the best part of the day." Even in the cold winter months, I enjoyed feeling like the first person in the world up and out. I didn't even mind the cold rain or snow at first, but I hated the tedious task of having to place the papers in plastic bags. It was fun for a while, and I made some money.

I even managed to have a little extra entertainment for myself while working. I rigged a makeshift sling for my pellet rifle on the rear bike fender. Originally, it was for those dogs that didn't like me riding through their yards at that hour. After the dogs got to know me, and didn't like the sting of the pellets, it became a great way to shoot the errant rabbit or squirrel I would come across. Sometimes, I would shoot them as I rode with no hands. I fancied myself shooting from the back of a horse the way they used to show the Indians shoot rifles from horseback in the old westerns. My kill ratio wasn't good enough to put food on the table, but I had a blast doing it.

Unfortunately, I didn't clear what money I thought I would. Once a month I had to go collecting. I dreaded it. It was amazing the excuses people could come up with for not paying up for the papers they just *had* to have before breakfast. Some would even shut off the blaring TV when I would ring the doorbell on collection evenings to make me think they weren't home.

It soured me a little, because I had to pay the distributor for my papers monthly. I was doing only about half as well as my friend said he was when I took the route.

My dad wouldn't let me quit, though. He would say things like, "You started it; now finish it. Never, ever quit anything."

Words of wisdom, for sure, but I was disappointed. I kept at it until I managed to sell another kid on the glories of the early morning hours. I would, however, remember the people who wouldn't pay.

The way I "remembered" them would eventually help send me off to a very different way of life.

CHAPTER 6

Busted

My friend Steve's parents allowed him to fix up their garage into a really cool pad. His dad got him a parachute from his squadron, and we hung it up in the ceiling. We backlit it with colored lights, along with some blacklight psychedelic posters of Woodstock and Playboy centerfold girls. We put a stereo in there and hung a few of our model planes. We got some crappy couches and furniture from neighbors who moved away. Yeah, we even had the mandatory lava lamp, too.

A real macho hangout, we saw it as just like the ones down at the squadron hangars we occasionally glimpsed during air shows and open houses squadrons would host for the public.

Naturally, it became a hangout for all of us teens in the neighborhood. We would have parties in there. Girls were starting to be very interesting to all of us, and they would come over too. Spin-the-bottle and a watered-down version of strip poker would sometimes take place when parents weren't around. Music from bands like Led Zeppelin, Steppenwolf, Iron Butterfly, Three Dog Night, and Jimmy Hendrix would fill the room. Those were considered the "head bands" of those days.

Our pad also attracted teens who were starting to experiment with marijuana, LSD, and speed. I didn't try any of it, though. I was too scared of my dad, who I just knew would know somehow. I was, however, really starting to dig the music. I was rebelling gradually and could relate to the vibe in the songs. Of the girls who came to those parties, some I liked and even won a kiss or two from during spin-the-bottle. Sometime during this phase, I got the notion it would be really fun to sneak out at night with my little crowd.

The first time, I tried it by myself. I had gone to bed on a Friday night. It was a beautiful spring night. My window was open to let in the cool night air. As I lay there, I heard what sounded like some Led Zeppelin tunes being played at high volume, carried on the breeze from somewhere down the street. I went to the window and listened, then realized it was a band playing down at the base pool. I *had* to go see what it was all about.

I quietly removed the screen, climbed out the window, and stepped out on top of the garage. I tiptoed ever so lightly across the roof. My parents were still up as I shimmied down a tree within reach. I peeked in through the window. They were watching TV, so I figured I had time to hop on my bike and pedal down to where all the fun was.

The sound got louder as I approached, pulling me toward it like a moth to flame. In those days minors had a base curfew. No one under eighteen was allowed to run around after 10 p.m. I knew this, but I was driven by the thrill and allure of getting close to that music.

As I rode up to the pool, I kept myself out of sight of the constantly roving MPs who liked to bust kids and take them home.

I watched from concealment. The crowd was mostly young officers from the BOQ (Bachelor Officer's Quarters) and their girls having a blast dancing, drinking, and throwing each other in the pool.

The band, from what I remember, was really good, sounding just like the records we were all listening to. I stayed for about an hour and rode home to a dark house. I climbed back up the tree, crossed over to the roof, and soundlessly entered my room. I didn't sleep much that night; my mind was racing with all sorts of fun we could get into after hours.

"Just wait till your mom and dad go to bed and I will come and throw a pine cone at your window and let's try it," I said the next day to my buddy, Howard. The next night came and I followed the same roof-to-tree routine and got Howard out. We just rode around on our bikes that night, having fun knowing we were out when none of our other friends could be.

The fun was just too much to keep to ourselves, and before long six or seven of us were out and about. It became sport to provoke and hide from the MPs, whether on foot or on our bikes. We knew every inch of the woods, river shoreline, and neighborhood. The MPs chased us many nights, but we lost them on foot one night.

"Cave!" I remember yelling as we ran through the woods.

That was a little hideout we had dug out of the side of the riverbank. It was quite the affair. The soil had a lot of clay in it, so it held together well. We dug a small, but concealable opening halfway up the side of perhaps a twenty-foot bank, maybe forty yards back from the water. We excavated a large room we could all nearly stand up in. It was a great place to go drink beer, smoke cigarettes, and try to coax girls into. We didn't have much luck with the girls, though, and it could get pretty muddy in the winter. No one but our inner circle knew where it was.

Under hot pursuit, we split up, and one by one reunited there. Man, we were proud of ourselves. We thought we were such bad-asses. This led us to start taunting the cops whenever we were out. We started pulling pranks, like starting people's lawn mowers in the middle of the night, just to hide and watch the bewildered resident come out with a "WTF?" look on his face. It was hilarious.

Things progressed the way mischievous things always do. They got worse.

We wound up stealing a car. Howard, who was now sixteen, had a learner's permit, which gave us permission to graduate from bikes to cruising around in a car. We were joined by another friend, Ray, who lived over in another section of MOQ (Married Officer's Quarters) in the apartment housing.

We all got out that night, quickly rode through the dark on our bikes, and with Ray serving up the keys, we "borrowed" his dad's Chevy Corvair. It was beat-up and really noisy, but the logic was, since it was parked in an apartment complex, no one would take notice when we cranked her up. No one did, and off we went, whooping like banshees.

We pulled this little stunt quite a few times, and when we were able to get some girls out to ride around with us—God, we thought we were kings. Some of the gang started to bring liquor . . . and some would bring pot.

I would drink some, but was still scared of the other stuff. I would take a joint from somebody and act like I was taking a hit, but really blowing out on it. That would make the end glow like I was really smoking, so I didn't have to endure any peer pressure. I don't think I fooled anybody, but no one ever said anything.

What idiots, we were.

We were underage in a stolen car, in possession of marijuana, involved in a possible DUI accident—or worse— all on federal property. We didn't have a care in the world. Ignorance. I shudder now. When I look back on it, we thought we were absolutely bulletproof. But, alas, we weren't. Like most juvenile delinquents, we eventually got caught.

It happened during the time my dad, who was the commanding officer of NARF (Naval Air Rework Facility), was thinking about retirement. He had just lost his medical clearance to fly. His years of hard living had caught up to him, and losing flying status really did a number on him. He also wasn't the same gung-ho warrior he was when he left for Vietnam. He came back a very changed man. The handcuffs that stupid politicians put on the military to fight the war their way—and still do—rather than effectively, the way the military is supposed to conduct wars, made it all for naught in the end. I think losing many of his friends needlessly because of the ridiculous micro-managerial ROE (Rules of Engagement) enforced by the Washington war planners, the escalation of the war by crony politicians to only better serve their greed, plus the treatment that so many servicemen and women received in the media and in public when they came home, really soured him. He was from the World War II generation, a war fought and won for a true reason, leading to victory, ticker-tape parades, and appreciation from a grateful nation.

It could have been that way for him and countless others if only the clique of politicians, bankers, and media had kept their meddling, manipulating hands out of things.

I truly believe that war should have been won quickly and decisively, or could have been avoided altogether. Instead, the usual suspects, in the same way as they do nowadays, would continually fuel a bloodbath ending the lives of more than 58,000 young American men and women for the sake of getting rich. Perhaps the anti-war movement may have had a point here, after all. Dad didn't want to keep being a part of things that had changed so much for the worse. He didn't care one iota about a desk job, either. That was prison for him. So, after thirty-five years of turnin' and burnin', I think he had finally had enough.

He and my mother started going down to South Carolina to look at property that suited their retirement plans. He would take some leave, and they would make long weekends out of it.

They would leave me in charge of the house and the pets. I was old enough for the responsibility . . . or so they thought. The minute they would leave, it was party time. I would immediately pick up the phone and start planning, and ready access to their liquor cabinet fired things up.

We would start drinking and go out and pull pranks all over the neighborhood, often doing damage to other people's property. This is when I would remember the people who wouldn't pay me for my newspaper delivery.

We tore stuff up, punctured tires, found very creative things to do with spray paint, and pulled the old burning-bag-of-shit trick—among other things. I was turning into a real punk. I am not proud of any of it now, but at the time it was so fulfilling, just to be a part of what I thought was an elite crew flying close to the sun. I imagine Icarus must have felt the same way right before the wax melted.

One of us even caused a bomb scare at school. The perpetrator never got caught. We all stood around smirking as the police came and went through the school, the whole student body out on the baseball field, wondering just who would have the balls to do that sort of thing.

Trouble in Shangri-La came in on the heels of glory, though. One morning, while cleaning up the house from the night's shenanigans before my parents got home from South Carolina, I noticed my allowance money, plus some cash I had made mowing lawns, was missing from where I had stashed it in the kitchen. After searching everywhere, I realized somebody must have taken it.

Feeling the sting of being stolen from, I grew hotter and hotter. I called the guys I figured would be the culprits, but nobody fessed up. I knew at least two of them were lying and that pushed me over the edge. And then, I did a really dumb thing.

I called base CID (Central Investigation Division).

The investigator listened very intently to what I told him. "We will work on this for you," he said. He asked me things like "Which quarters do you live in?

Who is your father?" and "Where do you go to school?" He also asked who it was I thought took the money.

I was never a tattletale in school. I never ratted anybody out, even when I had the goods on them. If they wronged me, I chose patience to even the score. The opportunity always comes up sooner or later, you know, like throwing a desk on somebody.

Or writing a book.

Well, this time I felt I had given them a chance to return the money to me— hell, we were all buzzed that night, and I figured they were pranking me at first— but they lied and didn't. So, I had no remorse about ratting them out. Self-righteous me, by God, was going to even the score.

 The same detective called me at home after school a few days later, asked a few more questions, and hung up. About a month went by, everything kind of quieted down for a bit with the sneaking out at night. We did, however, find one last way to seal our fate. Night was our friend, and we should not have abandoned her. We got pinched in broad daylight.

My little boat I had in Beaufort while Dad was in Vietnam made the move with us back to Cherry Point. I kept it down at the docks on nearby Hancock Creek. When we weren't looking for trouble, my friends and I would use it to fish, frog gig, explore, and sometimes camp out on weekends.

One Saturday afternoon, Karl, Steve, and I were out looking for a new place to fish. We found a little backwater that led right up to the end of one of the runways. We sat in the boat, fishing forgotten, thrilling at the sight of the A-6s and F-4s that were landing on that runway. The tail hook, flaps, landing gear, and bombs seemed to just graze our heads as they whooshed over, touching down a mere fifty yards or so from our vantage point. It was spectacular. Did I mention bombs? Yep.

We had another stroke of genius. I knew where there was an ammo dump not far off the slew we had motored up into. I said to Steve, "Man-o-man, wouldn't it be cool if we had one of those bombs sitting in the corner by the couch in your pad?"

Steve replied with some smartass comment like, "Sure man, just reach up and grab one off the next jet that comes in."

"No, I'm serious," I said. "I know where we can get one!"

He looked at me for a moment as though he either wanted no part of it, or I was just batshit crazy. I bet he soon wished he had stuck with the former because that day, unbeknownst to us at the time, would be the last day of freedom for all of us for a long, long time.

We pushed the boat back into the water and motored out to Hancock Creek. Turning right, away from the marina, I headed about a half mile back up the creek.

There, the woods on either side became dense and a little more foreboding, sort of the same way how either side of the river looks in the movie Apocalypse Now.

There were big signs on the left bank printed in bold red and yellow letters saying things like, TRESSPASSING BEYOND THIS PERIMETER IS EXPRESSLY FORBIDDEN, THIS AREA IS UNDER THE COMMAND OF SO-AND-SO OF THE SUCH-AND-SUCH ORDNANCE GROUP, LIVE EXPLOSIVES, DO NOT ENTER—USE OF DEADLY FORCE AUTHORIZED, and so on.

I beached the boat just upstream of these signs. We belly-crawled up the embankment to where I knew the ammo dump was. There beyond the hilltop, barely visible through the foliage, stood a guard shack beside a low fence surrounding all sorts of aviation ordnance: drop tanks, boxes of 20mm cannon shells, and just inside the wire, several bright-yellow painted bombshells. I knew these dummy bombs were not fused, but rather used for practice out on the various bombing ranges nearby. They only simulated the weight of their lethal brethren. Those, thank heavens, probably lay buried or were held in a much more secure location for the real fight going on in South East Asia.

The light was in our faces as we crept farther toward our objective. We should have aborted right there. The sunshine dappling the ground would make us that much more visible to the two sentries we observed sitting inside the guard shack. The lust for that centerpiece for our pad overrode common sense, however.

I was the smallest and fastest—I could really run in those days. My buddies called me "Mach 2" because I could really fly. Running from the MPs all the time can make your feet as fast as Mercury after a while.

This dubious honor selected me to go under the fence, grab the bomb, haul ass back down to the creek, load our prize, and boogie in the boat. My heart was beating like a jackhammer as I crawled under the low wire and reached the bomb I had picked out from our hiding place. I lay there behind some crates of shells and supplies for about ten minutes, just listening for any activity coming from the guard shack. Everything remained quiet, so I figured we were still undetected. There was no other way to get the bomb out of the enclosure but to grab it and run. It was only about ten feet from where I lay. It had to be in that pad. It belonged there, by God!

I took a deep breath—scared shitless, but committed now. I rose to a crouch, ran over, and grabbed my prize. It was heavy. I ran to the fence, tossed it over. I dove under the fence, came up running with the bomb in both hands on my way back to the boat. I almost made it.

Out of nowhere, I heard the heavy footsteps of one of the guards chasing me. Worse, he was gaining on me because of the heavy payload I was carrying with both hands.

The others, now realizing we were in a hell of a pickle, were running, too. We had nowhere to meet up later, nor had we planned for that.

"Halt! Now!" I heard from about ten yards behind me. "Stop! Now! Or you will be fired upon!"

I was beginning to realize I'd better stop. An NCO who could have been a linebacker for the Pittsburgh Steelers tackled me. We rolled up in a ball with him coming out on top of me, my face crammed in the dirt. Before I could mutter a muffled, "Oh Shit," he had his knee in my back slapping on the handcuffs.

The others had disappeared over the bank as I went down. I didn't know where anybody was, but I knew I was in a heap of trouble.

He jerked me to my feet by the handcuffs—this really hurts, by the way— and roared, "Just what the hell do you think you're doing, you little punk?" He turned me around and marched my now-very-small ass back toward the guard shack. I will spare some of the colorful names he called me.

When we got inside, he said, "Sit your damn ass down in that chair; don't move or speak." I was in the bracelets, and the other guy had an M-16 at the ready. I sat there like a statue, quiet as a mouse, with the funny feeling that I was going to die in approximately a minute.

"ID please," he said curtly. I handed over my base ID, which dependents were required to carry at all times while on base. These cards contain your name, address, and—most importantly—who your father is.

After he read that information, he sort of chuckled and said, "Well, well, well, the Colonel ain't gonna be happy today, is he boy?"

It turned out the ammo dump was part of my dad's command over at NARF. The guy in charge of the ammo dump reported directly to him. The guard picked up the phone and made the call that would change the course of my life

Just then, Steve and Karl burst through the door, white as ghosts, behind them two other M-16-toting guards. They had been caught soon after down at the creek bank. We must have been spotted long before we thought we were.

What on earth were we thinking? That we could sneak up on some combat-hardened Marines, probably just back from Vietnam and used to watching the woods for Charlie? Gawd! The mind of a teenager failed us—again!

My dad got the call and told the NCOs to bring us in to base CID (Central Intelligence Division). It wasn't a pleasant trip. They stuffed us into the covered bed of an MP truck, one just like the many we had arrogantly outrun many nights before. It was cramped and hot. We were locked in, and there were no windows. Rivers of sweat poured down my face. The handcuffs were eating into my wrists, sending bolts of pain up my arms whenever we would hit a bump in the dirt road leading out of the place. The driver made sure we hit every bump.

I was fifteen, and I was in big trouble. I was terrified of what Dad was going to do. His son was caught stealing potentially explosive ordinance from a military installation under his command. Jeeez. I was as good as dead.

Karl, Steve, and I were finally released from the handcuffs and were interrogated in separate rooms at CID for several hours. They sent us home to our parents.

I got a size-eleven boot up my rear end, walking in the door with a crying mother in the house. She was crying out of disappointment in me. I don't know which was worse: the ass whipping I got from my father, who was enraged like I had never seen before, or how hurt my mom was. I felt like shit to say the very least.

I went to my room and just sat there, feeling lower than a snake's belly in a wagon-wheel rut. I had to go to school the next day. I wasn't feeling very tough at all—more embarrassed than anything, now that I'd had a brush with how the big boys play.

The next day, coming home from school, I noticed a dark-blue car in the driveway. The sign on the door read, "Dept. of Defense—US Navy—For Official Use Only."

Oh boy, I thought. They have come to take me away to Leavenworth. Inside sat my parents with an investigator from CID.

My friends and I had thought the heat was dying down concerning our after-hours pranks, vandalism, and other miscreant behavior; but they had put two and two together. After the ammo dump bust, they realized we were the ones wreaking so much havoc—sneaking out after hours—around the neighborhood.

The option for me at this point was a juvenile record or military school. I guess by today's standards, all us boys would have been locked up in an institution of some kind. The investigator said if I chose the military-school option, there would be no charges filed. Without an ounce of bravado left in my deflated punk-ass ego, I took the smart choice for once in my life and said, "Military school."

About a week later, I was still intimidated, but a little defiance was starting to creep back into my soul, and I managed a few comments to my mom like, "I'm not going," or, "You can't make me go." I would never say anything like that to Dad, of course.

My mother very shrewdly and calmly said, "The one we picked out for you offers flight training if you can keep your grades up." Out of all the darkness in my life sprang a glimmer of hope and excitement. After all, I had been dreaming of flying since I was old enough to walk.

Hmmm, maybe this wouldn't be so bad after all.

CHAPTER 7

Reveille

I went off to military school. The want of learning to fly won out over any rebel-without-a-clue identity I held in my heart. My folks dropped me off at the Information and Documentation Center (INDOC), where you say your goodbyes to family or to whomever brings you there. No contact with the outside world was allowed for the next six weeks, except for emergency. For once, I didn't feel cocky.

"Hang in there. Keep your grades up and remember our deal," Mom said along with other words of encouragement.

I was facing being really alone for the first time. Lots of tough kids from different places and backgrounds loomed all around me, which was pretty rough on a 15-year-old four-eyes who thought he was somebody.

The first stop was the barbershop, which offered one style—buzz-cut. Long hair was the thing with teenagers then, and I had some locks, but it took only about four broad swipes with the electric razor for them to disappear.

Feeling like Sampson now, I processed through uniform and PT clothes issue, and got assigned to a company. The student body consisted of four companies, all structured just like the military. Each divided into platoons and squads.

The campus was a somewhat-renovated World War II Army Air Corps training base that had become part of the local airport. The field now-historic had been used to train kids not much older than me to fly, fight, and die in the skies over Europe and the Pacific during World War II. It hadn't changed that much. To say the least, things were very spartan as far as creature comforts went.

I drew Band Company and got assigned to a squad leader, usually a corporal or sergeant, who had been there at least the year before, and who had earned rank. My arms fully loaded with clothing and classroom supplies, I felt rather small, sporting my new buzz cut. I reported to my squad leader. I walked up the stairs into the Band Company barracks. They really were barracks, not dorms like most places have now. I walked past the cadet NCO posted at the door and asked for the squad leader.

First mistake.

He slammed me up against the wall. "No one!" he yelled. "No one! *Especially* maggot new boys, ever walks past the OG (Officer of the Guard)—or anyone else with rank here—without asking permission to continue! Got it?"

He had me do twenty-five push-ups, after which I snapped to attention. He certainly had my attention at this point. I asked the required permission to continue and went in search of my contact.

I found him. He assigned me to my bunk and showed me how to organize my locker, a wooden trunk underneath the bed, which would be inspected almost every day along with every area that I was responsible for. At this point, that included my locker, my bunk, and me. Yes, the upper classmen would do the quarter flip on the bunk thing just like at Annapolis or West Point.

The first week before classes started was very challenging. I got my share of hazing in one form or another, did lots of push-ups, and scrubbed lots of latrines with toothbrushes, but somehow survived. Everybody else was getting the same exact treatment, so it wasn't like I was being singled out.

We lived by the bugle call. They had one for everything—one for getting up in the morning, for morning PT, eating, time to go to class, lunch, end of class, afternoon drill, evening meal, study hall, and one to have your ass in the rack at night on time.

Little by little, I fell into the rhythm of it all while doing my best to stay out of trouble from older boys with rank. I started to take some pride in keeping my bunk and uniform in top shape and looking sharp. I did my best at PT and schoolwork. I actually was making a few friends amongst us "maggots" too.

By the fourth week, not worried so much about being away from home, I sort of liked the tight schedule. The thing I wasn't good at was being in Band Company. The other companies were called "Rifle Companies." No, we weren't training to go to Vietnam yet, although a few seniors who graduated in '71 did serve with distinction, but it was all over in 1972. Nonetheless, each of the guys in these other units had been issued an M-14 rifle, a real one, sans firing pin.

Assigned to Band Company, I didn't get an M-14. I was issued, of all things, a snare drum. My job was to learn the parade cadence and music for the other companies to march by. Ironically, I just couldn't play the damn thing or remember the cadence. Maybe I didn't really want to. A sort of envy of the guys in the rifle companies was developing in me. One thing was sure: my future was not the drums. The rifle companies were a little tougher on the maggots, but in a way that made them just a little more elite to me somehow. They seemed a little more military.

My God! What could be happening to the proud punk here? I thought. I knew I was about to wash out of the drum line and probably get some laughable slot as cymbal player or worse, so I put in for a transfer to Bravo Company—a rifle company, and got accepted.

Bravo Company was commanded by a senior who held the rank of Captain.

Chris was one of the most charismatic natural leaders I have ever known. As I got to know him, I learned what real loyalty, camaraderie, and purpose was all about. The guy could really inspire people. Even at just eighteen years of age, he had the most well-disciplined, sharpest unit on campus, with the highest morale. He was no pushover by any means, but he had the talent to make people want to do for him and to be a part of something, like making Bravo Company the coveted Best-all-Around company.

The units were judged on everything from demerit levels, grades, and barracks' appearance to parade and drill performance. Intramural sports counted, too, although my contributions weren't too good in that area, except for track. I could still run like a jackrabbit. I found myself full of pride taking care of my weapon, my bunk space, my appearance, and through some of his encouragement, even my grades. We won Best-all-Around every month that year, by the way.

My parents came to the school's first dress parade for families at the end of the six weeks. It was a beautiful Sunday afternoon. After the parade, the battalion was dismissed for some free time with families. There must have been some kind of change for the better in me, because my mom's tears were from joy. And Dad, after he saw how I carried myself in uniform and how clean my M-14 looked, well . . . let's just say he had that twinkle in the eyes.

Within another month I managed to stay sharp, keep out of trouble, and got my first promotion. My name made the list for PFC (Private First Class)— "mosquito wings," as we called the insignia back then. I can't even begin to tell you how good it felt to pin those little stripes on my collar.

I maintained a B average, light years from my public-school grades of all F's, and true to word, my folks made good on me getting to start the flying-lesson program. My chest was starting to puff out a little bit now, but for the all the right reasons. Maybe flunking out of band because I couldn't play a snare drum was for the best.

My very first flying lesson, I did really well. The basics just came naturally to me. Maybe it was because I had read everything I could get my hands on regarding the subject. I like to think I just had it in my blood.

Quite pleased, the instructor told me I would have no problems getting to solo. After nine hours of dual instruction, teaching me how not to kill myself, we taxied back to the ramp one day. I was expecting to shut down the engine as usual, but I was in for a surprise. "It's all yours," he said as he stepped out of the plane, "Take it up, stay in the pattern and land it three times." I started grinning uncontrollably from ear to ear. He shut the door and stepped back as I taxied off.

I wasn't nervous at all. As I took off and climbed to altitude, I remember being very much at peace. Everything my instructor had taught me flowed through my brain, and I found myself really enjoying the better performance from the aircraft. The only anxiety was self-induced because I wanted to make three of the prettiest landings anyone at the airport had ever seen.

With the landings accomplished, although not as perfect as I wanted, I taxied back to the ramp with an undamaged airplane and me still sporting that mile-wide grin. I had just turned sixteen and thought I was pretty hot stuff.

Still, I had much to learn.

As a fledgling pilot, I still had a lot of work ahead of me in order to qualify for every pilot's first milestone: the Private Pilot Certificate. As mentioned before, myriad requirements must be fulfilled. I had to log a few more hours solo, flying around locally or just staying in the traffic pattern practicing my landings in various conditions.

I was on my way!

CHAPTER 8

Runnin' On Empty

The next step in my flying protocol was cross-country navigation. It started with minimal ground school time, followed by a trip with an instructor to a different airport about a hundred miles away. The instructor I did my first solo flight with had since left town for a better job, so I was assigned to another. I don't think this man's heart was in teaching. He was pretty old, and he seemed very detached. Sometimes while aloft, I would look over at him, thinking he seemed awfully quiet, and he would be sound asleep. In ground school, he briefly explained the basics of dead-reckoning navigation, but that was about it. In those days, long before GPS became available, that was about all we had—a compass, a clock, and a topographical map to mark a course and progress toward a destination.

I had more to learn, of course, like VOR (Very High Frequency Omni-Range), a nationwide system of ground-based radio transmitters that allowed a pilot to track a specific course to and from the station, and ADF (Automatic Direction Finding), another ground-based system that caused the receiver needle in the aircraft to always point to the transmitter. I didn't get any instruction on these features from my disengaged instructor. I felt incredibly ill-prepared when he sent me off on my very first cross-country flight.

The night before, I diligently did all my prep work and planned the trip up to Cheraw, South Carolina. It was only about a fifty-minute hop, and I was excited. That next day I pre-flighted the airplane, had the instructor look over my prep work, and filed the flight plan with the FSS (Flight Service Stations.) I was to depart at 1100.

I climbed into the cockpit, then organized my map, notes, and the old slide-rule computer called an E6B. The E6B was all anyone carried in those days before iPads and apps. Even the jet pilots used them. It's a fascinating device, like a slide rule, only round. It can perform all the calculations any computer can today. You just had to do it manually by moving the numbers around the dial.

I fired up the engine, checked the fuel and other items one last time, taxied out to the runway, and took off. Climbing out, I felt really good to finally be going somewhere. It was fall, so the weather was exceptionally clear—"severe clear," as flyers like to call it. With the cool temperatures, my little plane and I made it to our cruising altitude of 4500 feet in no time.

I had my map folded in such a way that the course line I drew between Camden and Cheraw was at my fingertips. I had numerous checkpoints highlighted along that course line for reference, like I had been taught. Using my trusty E6B, I had carefully figured the drift correction and compass heading that I would fly to maintain course all the way to Cheraw. I settled in my seat, feeling great.

The sky was vivid blue. The whole state of South Carolina seemed to lie at my feet like a vast patchwork quilt bathed in sunshine. Camden was receding rapidly behind me. The engine was purring, all gauges in the green, and my checkpoints were sliding under the wings right on time. The slipstream whooshing by the window sounded so good. I felt vibrantly alive, totally free, and not of this world, all its troubles left far below. What could possibly go wrong at this point?

Plenty.

After I marked off around my fourth checkpoint on the map, I noticed I didn't see the next one about the time my E6B calculations said I would. I checked the map and could see where the crosswind appeared to be a little stronger than forecast. I made a correction that I thought would get me back on course. I wasn't worried. There was a big river just to the north of Cheraw and I figured if I got to the river, I could follow it to the airfield not far away.

Here's where I could have used that instruction in radio-aids to navigate. If I had known and understood how simple it was to use them to pinpoint your position and navigate by, I might not have turned a simple fifty-minute flight into something far more serious.

The farther north I flew that day, the stronger-than-forecast the wind became. I eventually got to the river, but nothing on my map matched up. I endlessly flew up and down the river looking for that airport.

No luck.

I tried calling them on the radio.

No answer.

The airplane I was flying was a little two-seater 1970 Cessna 150. I still remember its tail number: N60578.

The pilot's handbook on this particular airplane states that with a full load of fuel, one can stay airborne for close to four hours.

Well, by now I was becoming more than a little frustrated. I was well into hour three on the fuel. Both gauges, now below a quarter full each, seemed to be rapidly moving toward empty with each furtive glance.

If I can't find the damn airport, I am going to have to ditch this thing in a field or something, I thought.

If you have time to pick just the right spot, the landing in such a field is usually survivable—but sometimes not. Once you pick one and have a dead engine, you are committed. Things like power lines, ditches, livestock, and holes don't always show up from the air. They can really ruin your day. Regardless, you stick with what you have set up for and try for the best.

I sat there thinking, *I'm only 16. I'm too young to die.* I was a little scared, but mostly mad as hell at myself for blowing my first solo cross-country.

The river lay below, meandering through its curves, unconcerned. It was the only thing I could match up on the map as to where I was.

Then, I remembered reading something a while back about a navigation aid to pilots in trouble, something called the DF (direction finder) steer. No, it's not a special breed of cow; it's a way for someone on the ground to find a wayward aircraft by the pilot using his voice radio transmitter. This service was provided when needed by Flight Service Stations (FSS). These stations were owned and staffed by the FAA. Facilities like these used to be all over the country, usually within two-hundred miles of each other. They provided various services to pilots like weather forecasting, a place to file your flight-plan, study materials, and a place to go take the various written tests. I had hoped that now they would provide me with my much-needed DF steer.

Based on where I thought I was, I figured the FSS station located in Florence, South Carolina, was about seventy-five miles away. I knew I had to climb higher to reach them on the radio. I knew it would take precious fuel to do so, but I was quickly running out of options.

I reached down, pushed the throttle forward, and began to climb. I leveled off at ten-thousand feet. The air was cold, the plane light, so it took little to no time to get there. The higher you go the more out of this world you feel. On a clear day such as this, the view was spectacular. For a minute or two, I found myself enjoying it, even though I was in a bind.

Oh well, I thought, *if I run outta gas and the engine quits, I'll have plenty of time to pick the best field to land in from this altitude.*

From my perch seemingly atop the universe, I dialed in the radio frequency for Florence FSS.

"Florence Flight Service, Cessna 60578 requesting a DF steer," I said into the mic. I waited for a response . . .

Silence.

I turned up the volume. Nothing but the hiss of static. I tried again. Still nothing. I tried a few more times with no luck. The fuel was getting low. I started to accept the fact I was going to have to pick out one of those fields below for an emergency landing.

"Aircraft calling Florence Flight Service, go ahead," finally came over the cockpit speaker.

Relieved, I transmitted back what I needed.

"Cessna 60578, roger. Please transmit a long count now," they said. A long count is where you count slowly from 1 to 10 and then 10 to 1. This allows them to get a bearing on your transmitter. If you have a general idea of where you are they can laterally pinpoint your position for you.

They found me and asked my destination.

"Cheraw Municipal," I said.

"Ugh, 578. Suggest heading two six two for 42 and that should put you on top of Cheraw. We have notified the airport there and they are monitoring Guard and Unicom. Give them a call in range." Guard is the international distress frequency and Unicom is the national common traffic advisory frequency used by local traffic at most non-towered airports.

I turned to that heading and glued the compass there. I pulled off the power to conserve fuel and started the long descent. I didn't notice it before, but it had become very cold in the cockpit from the high altitude.

At least that's what I told myself I was shivering from.

As I passed through eight-thousand feet, I heard, "Cessna 60578, how do you hear on Unicom?" It wasn't the same voice from FSS.

"Aircraft calling 60578; I hear you loud and clear," I said.

"578, go air to air," the voice commanded.

I spun the air-to-air frequency into the dial and said, "578's up."

Whoever it was came right back with "578, this is Bellanca four niner Whiskey. I'm in a decathlon based out of Cheraw and orbiting east of the field. We heard you earlier transmitting on Guard frequency. I launched to try and help find you. Tell me a prominent landmark you can see from your position, and I will fly to it. You can follow me in to Cheraw from there."

Chills ran up my spine. Not from being in a tight spot, but from the realization of the brotherhood I had joined. I had joined rather clumsily today, but nonetheless joined. Unexpected things can happen to anybody, and pilots will do just about anything to help out one another in trouble, no matter what.

I picked out a huge warehouse in a big clearing.

He saw it and started circling it.

Headed right for it, I spotted a tiny spec over the warehouse. It had to be him. "Four niner Whiskey, 578, got you in sight. I'm at your four o'clock."

After a second or two, he said, "Roger, I have you in sight. Follow me." I didn't know how to fly formation then, so I just fell in about a quarter-mile trailing behind him. We had about ten or fifteen miles to go at this point.

Oddly, the heading that FSS had given me wasn't close enough for me to have ever seen the airport. That little Decathlon in front of me was the prettiest thing I had ever seen; the fuel gauge needles resting right on top of the E were not.

I called the pilot on air-to-air and advised him of this.

He pointed out the field.

I saw it, and he peeled off, telling me to land first. I switched frequency to Unicom, announced my position and intentions to land. I didn't fly the pattern; I headed straight for the end of the runway. I held my breath the last few miles expecting the engine to conk out at any second. At low altitude, that would not have been a pretty sight.

I stayed as high as possible in order to give myself the best odds of making the runway if that engine should quit. Not far from the threshold, and still about a thousand feet above the ground, I chopped the power, rolled in full left aileron, and applied right rudder to the stop. This caused the plane to enter a slip. In a slip the plane falls like a rock because the relative wind is now flowing sideways over the wings, making them much less efficient. It's not dangerous as long as the aircraft's pitch attitude and airspeed are watched carefully.

I released the pressure on the controls, flared, and touched down about a third of the way down the strip. I coasted to the end and pulled off onto the taxiway, relief flooding over me. As I started to motor back towards the ramp of Cheraw Municipal, the engine suddenly coughed, sputtered, and died.

As the old saying goes, "I'd rather be lucky than good any day."

The Bellanca driver turned out to be a retired Air Force pilot turned civilian instructor at Cheraw. He landed, shut down his engine, and walked into the FBO where I was sitting.

Needless to say, I was feeling very stupid for having bungled such a simple mission. Back then, as a student pilot, you had to have your logbook signed by someone—preferably an instructor pilot—from the destination airport in order to prove you completed the trip.

He sat down with me and said, "I will sign your logbook, but as an instructor, I'm curious about why you think you got lost so badly."

I thought for a moment. "Well, I guess I didn't factor the increasing winds aloft, and they blew me farther off course than I realized."

"Why didn't you cross reference two VORs to find your position?" he asked.

I didn't understand the question. "Uh . . . I don't think I have been taught that part yet."

He was livid. "You mean to tell me your IP signed you off for cross country and didn't show you how to use VOR or ADF in addition to dead reckoning?" He was mad and reverting back into military mode.

"Yes, sir," was all I could manage.

"Who is your IP down there at Camden, son?" he asked.

I told him, and he went into the office and shut the door. I don't know who he called, maybe it was my instructor back in Camden, but from out in the lobby I could hear him yelling.

I busied myself with fueling the plane back up. I wasn't thrilled about the trip home and the possibility of getting lost again. Evening formation on campus was in less than two hours, and I had to be there or be AWOL. I would be in big trouble for that. The ex-Air Force pilot came out of the office, calmed down, and said, "Sit down here, son, and I'll show you a few tricks to get you back home."

We spread the map out on the table. He went over everything I should have known before I left Camden that morning. I wished he was my instructor. He made everything so easy to understand. I folded up the map, headed out to the plane now re-fueled and sitting ready.

He walked out with me, then sat in the cockpit for a few minutes to make sure I got what he showed me in the office. I thanked him over and over for literally saving my bacon. We shook hands, and I thanked him again. He just smiled, winked, and said, "Shake it off, kid; it happens to the best of us." He stood smoking a cigarette, leaning against the office door, watching me as I taxied out.

I took off and, with my newfound navigation skills using the proper tools, made it home in just under forty-five minutes. I would have some paperwork to fill out about overdue aircraft with Florence FSS, and a lot of explaining to do at Camden Airport. After I landed, I had about fifteen minutes until evening formation on campus.

After securing the airplane for the night, I changed from civvies back into uniform in seconds, then set off running to make formation in time. I called back over my shoulder that I would be back tomorrow for the paperwork.

I slid into formation, panting, but was standing in my spot before the bugle call ended. It struck me funny that all around me were kids finishing up the day of homework and sports activities, working off demerits, or just being bored stuck on campus with not much to do. No one had the slightest clue as to where I'd been, alone, high in the sky, over a hundred miles away, flirting with possible disaster. The scary stuff was now fading quickly, the way it always does in youth.

I marched into the mess hall for supper with the rest of the battalion, a little smirk curling around the edges of my face.

CHAPTER 9

Last Dance, First Glimpse

By my senior year, I had crawled up through the ranks, got on the dean's list, and made it into the officer level as first lieutenant with my own platoon. I didn't have to go back after my first year, but I was surprised to realize that I wanted to. I still managed to keep that little rebel spirit alive, though, but this time it was in a much healthier way.

Technically, no cadets in the student body were ever allowed to leave the campus except for emergencies, either medical or family. I had soloed my first airplane, but in order to fulfill the requirements for my private license, I had to log quite a few more hours flying cross-country flights. By now, my folks had retired from the Marine Corps and moved to a place out in the country about fifty miles from the airport where I learned to fly.

On Saturdays the entire battalion, except for those guys serving off demerits, had the day off. I would walk over to the airport, check out a plane, and fly east. I knew where the farm was, so I would just drop down low and buzz the house. This let my mom know I was on the way to the little grass strip all the crop dusters used, not far from there.

She would leave the house and come pick me up. I spent Saturdays at home just relaxing away from the campus for a while. I think she got a kick out of it, actually. She would say, "I remember doing things like this with your father, when he could sneak away for the weekend. Like father, like son, I guess."

As long as I was back in time for evening formation, no one ever questioned where I had been. They just thought I was working on my flying stuff. Was I breaking the rules? Yeah, maybe a little, but without the malice I used to live by a few years ago.

Toward the end of my senior year, I was looking forward to going to the senior prom. Music still fascinated me, and I was into all the popular bands. As fate would have it, it wasn't the only bug I caught. The night of the prom, I got the flu. I wasn't about to miss this event, however, because a friend of mine named Steve—not the same Steve from Cherry Point—had formed a band with some of the other cadets at school. I had met a local girl named Ginger and asked her to be my date for the prom. She accepted.

A senior at the public high school, Ginger looked very pretty. My plan was to show her the time of her life. So, off I went in a borrowed car to pick her up. I had only gotten my driver's license after turning eighteen a few days before. Up till then, I hadn't thought driving was very important.

We arrived to find the gym packed, full of cadets and their dates. The music blared through large speakers on each side of the stage. Some couples danced, others huddled around the punch bowl, and many simply sat awkwardly around the perimeter. I had intended to dance and romance with Ginger all night, but something happened that would change my life forever.

I was fascinated by the band's performace, especially the drumming by my friend, Steve. Like fishermen and sailors say about the sea, the stage was calling to me.

We made our way to the front. By now, it seemed like the whole student body was leaning against the stage, watching them more like a concert than a dance. I felt Ginger tug on my sleeve a couple of times, but I couldn't look away. I was mesmerized. The pull of the music, especially the drums, had me hypnotized, in a strange spell of sorts. This was no snare drum. This instrument could captivate an entire audience.

Watching Steve and the rest of the band, I thought, *I'm gonna do that!*

And just like that—*blam!* It was that simple, an epiphany. I was hooked for life.

I stayed in that spot until the dance ended and the band thanked the crowd. I finally turned my attention back to Ginger, but she was long gone. I guess she went home or perhaps found someone else to dance with. I felt a little bad about that, but I also felt excited knowing now what I wanted to do. As crazy as it seemed, especially after having attended four years of military school, I wanted to be a drummer.

I vowed to learn everything I could about it.

Military school was a great experience, all told. Many thanks to my parents for showing tough love way back before it was just a buzzword. They saved my life, really. I graduated in 1974. I did okay in the end, considering the shape I was in when I got there.

Out of the eight platoons there on campus, we scored first runner-up in best overall platoon at graduation. Graduation day was a blast. The field filled with cadets and parents, including mine. At the end of the ceremony, the last "Baaa-TALLLYYAUN . . . DiiiiiissMISSED!" came floating out over the parade ground. Hats and cheers flew into the air. We broke ranks for the last time, everyone saying goodbye and good luck.

There was a lot of, "Yeah, bro, I'll stay in touch." Of course, you never do, but that's the way it was.

I remember leaving that campus for the last time. It seemed then like a lifetime had already passed. I drove away with a wistful, reflective feeling of lots accomplished but with trepidation about leaving the life I had grown accustomed to. I was leaving for the outside.

It was the same trepidations I had when I reported to INDOC that first day, with so many bugle calls yet to learn.

CHAPTER 10

Bad Trip, Good Night

After military school, I tried my hand at being a college student at Francis Marion University in Florence, South Carolina. What I really wanted to do now, though, was be in a band. Whenever I was working, I was always saving money for drum stuff. When I wasn't working, I was either practicing or jamming with friends. It really wasn't a conscious effort. It *possessed* me.

My whole brain was occupied with getting somewhere with this thing, as many fellow musicians can easily relate. Many would agree with me that this possession could sometimes seem a curse. In many cases, it can prevent us from being able to focus on more productive things. I was still in love with airplanes, but I had to put my flying goals on hold. I just couldn't afford it right then. It seemed impossible to amass enough hours ever to make it into the airlines. With less than perfect eyesight, a military career was off the books. Aviation would lie dormant in me for several years, but it would always be there, coming back into play at a great time.

I would go to every club with a good band and study what the drummers would do, rather than focus on my schoolwork. I would go back to my living quarters, which was usually a dive, and practice what I saw until I got it.

When a major touring act would pass through the area, I would get tickets if I could afford them, sometimes driving many hours to see the show. The mystique surrounding the touring acts fascinated me. I would get as close as possible to the buses and trucks just for the vibe, and try to imagine what the people in the band were doing and thinking right before coming out to play for twenty-thousand of us wide-eyed fans. I would sit in my seat transfixed, staring down the sight line of the spotlight beams in the rafters hitting the performers down below. The same people in the pictures on my albums were right there. I soaked in the showmanship and attitude that it takes to play in the big leagues.

I was captivated both by the size of the buildings and by how small they could seem with crowd and band feeling the same thing in unison.

One night, a few friends and I drove from Florence up to Greensboro, North Carolina, to see the Doobie Brothers. The opening act was Mother's Finest. Their drummer, Barry Borden, to this day remains one of my favorites. I used to go see them play in the clubs all around Carolina when I could. When the house lights in Greensboro went down that night and the stage lights came up, there they were, exploding on stage, just like they did in the clubs, but in front of fifteen-thousand people. It was awesome even in the nosebleed section, seeing them own the house after being up close so many times in the clubs. I couldn't stand it; I needed to be closer. Just like years before, pulled toward that band playing at the base pool, I left my seat and wormed my way through the people standing on the floor, up to the very front of the stage.

By now the Doobies were rockin' the house and being right in front of the stage just wasn't enough. There weren't barricades back then like at concerts now. You could actually lean against the stage and watch the performance. It could get a little stuffy sometimes, but who cared? We were all there enjoying the same thing. Was I content with that? Nope. I wanted to feel what the band was feeling.

I raised myself up onto the stage. I didn't want to get close to any of the players or anything like that; I was just dying to see what it looked like on the other end of that spotlight beam. I wanted to look out over the crowd and get a glimpse of what it must be like to play for that many people loving you. A glimpse is all I got, because security grabbed me by the belt and collar and threw me out the back door.

I froze my ass off to say the least. I don't remember how I later found my friends that night, but they told me the show was great. I smiled. "Yeah? Well you guys got a great show, but I got a vision."

"You are going to be mine, someday," I whispered to nobody but the wall of the Carolina Coliseum in Columbia, South Carolina, one night as I pressed my hand against it. Fleetwood Mac had just finished a mind-blowing show there that night. I was standing on the balcony, overlooking the load-out activity below and the feeling came over me that my sentiments really would come true somehow.

Not long after that, another of my favorite bands was coming to the town where I lived, Florence, South Carolina. Tom and some others I hung out with were all going to the Charlie Daniels concert at Francis Marion. "We'll be thinking about you in the front row tonight, bro," Tom jeered at me.

"Yeah, whatever," I said.

Shit!

I wanted to go, but just couldn't afford it. I was getting by just by the skin of my teeth financially with rent, a beat-up '71 Ford Pinto, a low-paying part-time job, and trying to get by in school. Someone like Charlie coming to a little place like Florence was huge, to say the least. I was really down, though, because it was a show I definitely didn't want to miss. I loved Charlie's first major album, *Fire on the Mountain*. It's still one of my favorites today. Of course, I had learned to play along with all the songs on it, banging away on drums in my apartment—to the neighbors' dismay.

I felt like I was missing out. *Damn!* I thought, *of all the times to be broke.* The day of the show was electric. Kids were driving around with CDB music pouring out their car radios, partying, getting ready for the big event.

Tom was not a musician, but you could say he was an audiophile, for sure. He had every record you could imagine. He had a *great* stereo. Not a bad place to be sometimes. Anyway, he was what we called a "head" back then. He smoked a lot of dope. He must have been a pretty smart guy because he managed to stay in school with a three-point-something average.

He knew my passion for music, too. I guess he felt bad for me that night, because even though he knew I didn't smoke, he put a big fat joint in my hand and said, "Man, I'm sorry you can't go with us tonight; maybe this will help." I took it and held it in my hand, not really knowing what I should do with it as they drove away. I put it in my pocket and went back inside.

I sat there awhile, imagining how great the show was going to be, how I wasn't going to be there, and I started to feel sorry for myself. *Hell, why not? Think I'll just go light this thing up and find out what everybody thinks is so great about it.*

I got into my Pinto and drove to a little lake back in the woods where we all used to hang out, not far from the apartment. It was a beautiful moonlit night, still as a church on Monday.

I got out, leaned against the car and lit up. I didn't feel anything on the first couple of hits, so I took a few more . . . then some more . . . and then a little more, until I had burned the whole thing.

I ate the roach just like I had seen others do many times before. If I'm going to do something, I do it all the way.

Oh boy.

The skin on my head started to squeeze my skull. My hair started to slide backwards over my head and down into my collar. That quiet lake in the woods became a bright silver mirror, beckoning me to step out on it. Every tree surrounding it transformed into a major work of abstract art that held some deep relative meaning for me. A cacophony of noises—crickets chirping, a bird rustling in its nest, a dog barking off in the distance—all registered in my brain as loud as a gunshot. I could hear like a bat and felt wide-eyed as an owl. The moon started doing weird stuff like going in little circles. Then things started flying back and forth across it. It started moving around the sky, eating the stars just like the little Pac-Man dude would do with the dots.

Holy shit. What the hell!

Leaning against the car, I felt like my weight against it was beginning to push it sideways towards the ditch. Something told me I better get to the apartment *quick*, so I got back into the car and sat there trying to remember how to start it.

After accomplishing that monumental feat of coordination, I very cautiously crept along the dirt road back to the pavement. Driving back, it took all the con-centration I could muster just to keep going. I thought I was driving way too fast for the curves until I would look at the speedometer reading ten miles an hour. I actually felt like I was someone else, sitting in the *passenger* seat, watching this really goofy guy try to operate a machine that was *way* above his grasp.

Somehow, I got back to the parking lot, parked, and turned on the radio. What was on at the moment? Yep. Charlie Daniels. I heard things in the music I had never heard before. It was so vivid, so colorful. With all the subtle phrasing in the arrangements suddenly becoming obvious, it was like CDB was painting a tapestry just for me to see, touch, and relate to. That did it. I was going to the show!

With the campus in walking distance of my apartment, I figured if nothing else I could just go stand outside the building and hear a little, or catch the vibe somehow. I started the journey. From walking to class, I knew the quickest way, or thought I did. A fifteen-minute walk turned into about a forty-five minute trek across "No Man's Land."

The enhanced sights and sounds had turned into paranoia. I don't know why, but the buzz just sort of suddenly shifted gears. I just knew someone was follow-ing me. I hid in the ditch and waited to cross the highway until no cars could see me. I thought they would just know I was high and would probably call the cops.

I finally scurried across the highway and ran to the sanctuary of the trees on the other side. There I crept from trunk to trunk, stopping at each one, waiting for whomever or whatever was pursuing me to show themselves. *How do people enjoy this shit?* I wondered. I was scared out of my head. It was very real. Forget about the moon, mirrors, and beckoning music on the radio; I was being hunted.

I got out of the trees and kept heading toward the concert hall across the open campus grounds. Now I was falling back to my days running from the base MPs. I used every shadow, every bush, and every parked car to my advantage.

Whatever was after me pushed me toward the relative safety of a crowd of people.

At last, with my heart in my throat, I got around the backside of the Student Center where the concert was going on. The opening act, Grinderswitch, was finishing their last song and, through the back door, I could get a peek at some of the colored lights above the stage. Or maybe they weren't colored . . .

I hung out there by the door, gradually forgetting about the boogeyman as I listened to Grinderswitch finish up and heard the crowd roar. What was I going to do now? I was still paranoid, but it was fading somewhat. So, I just stood there trying to maintain a low profile.

Suddenly, the doors sprang open. Students and road-crew types were pushing cases and carrying instruments out the door and loading them into the opening act's bus. It was that sudden flurry of activity that snapped me out of my trance. Someone left a microphone stand parked by the door, so I impulsively snatched it and walked in. I carried it like it was important to somebody at the moment and no one stopped me.

I walked right into the side stage area and started acting like I was working. I moved a few cases around just trying to look busy until the lights would go down, and I could ease my way into the house and see the show. It worked. I gradually wound up in front of the stage, of course.

The best part, though, was seeing the expression on my friend Tom's face when we made eye contact while I was backstage *working*. His jaw dropped. I winked and flipped him the bird. We both laughed, but I put my finger up to my lips like, "Shhhh."

After the show, the crazy hallucinogenic buzz had worn off, and I damn sure didn't want any more of that. I told him how I got in.

I think we must have laughed for hours.

CHAPTER 11

Beginner's Luck

College offered a new world full of adventure.

I had an experience with a young lady that, although rather terrifying at the time, worked out to be a blessing in disguise. From childhood to my early teen years, I was so focused on learning to fly that I didn't spend much time perfecting my backseat skills with the girls like some of my friends did—or so they claimed. I had my fair share of crushes, but I never could muster the courage to talk to those aloof, untouchable goddesses. They always seemed to be interested in the sports guys anyway, so I figured, *What the hell, one will come along someday and all that will take care of itself.* Although that was a nice thought, it wasn't exactly how my first brush with romance played out.

For a while, I lived in student housing across the highway from FMU. I had a second-storey efficiency apartment there. It wasn't much, but most of my neighbors were students, as well, and we all hung out there after classes. Some good parties sprung up around the pool in warmer weather, and sometimes those parties would retire to someone's apartment to continue well into the wee hours of the morning. My apartment won the honors one night, and what a night it turned out to be.

I was nineteen years old. It was springtime, and I would be twenty in about a month. By today's standards—and probably then, too—it was really late in life to still be a reluctant virgin. But, as I previously mentioned, I was bashful to a fault.

The little group I was hanging with ended up in my apartment, all laughing, drinking, and having a blast. I had the tunes cranked on the stereo and the night was young. I wound up at the kitchen table shooting tequila with three or four friends and a girl I had not seen hanging around the housing complex before. She was really cute and seemed to like the bravado and charm the tequila was giving me. We started playing cards. The rest of the gaggle of drunken college kids who weren't at the table started to drift off to other parties, or back to their own cribs. It got down to just one other couple and me—and the new girl.

Her name was Beth. She was from somewhere up north and had traveled a lot. I had just enough of a buzz going from the tequila that I didn't pick up on the red flags. The hormones were raging, too, so even if I had been drinking only water, I doubt any red flags would have been seen. As we sat ogling each other in facing chairs, the card game forgotten, the others figured it would be a good time to leave us, so they split. I remember realizing we were alone, and my heart leaping at the possibilities. We talked and flirted. I decided it's now or never, and I kissed her as she fell into my arms.

Sometime after midnight, our teenage love/lust depleted, a horrendous pounding started on my apartment door. It sounded like a battering ram. Roused from my endorphin-saturated bliss of newly found manhood, I felt the first pangs of fear begin to grip my heart.

The first thing I thought was that Beth had lied to me about her age and all the places she had been, and she was a local underage girl trying to hang with the older crowd. It must be her dad beating the door down.

Oh. My. God!

I went to the peephole. What I could see turned the fear pangs into hot knives. Outside stood a guy as tall as the doorframe and almost as wide, dressed in Hells Angels-style clothes. I saw him turn and say something to somebody else, just as he drew back his melon-sized fist to pound the door again. I could see about five others, big and dressed the same way under the porch light, the convex peephole distorting their shapes into gargoyles.

Trying to sound as tough as I could, I managed, "Whaddya want? It's one o'clock in the damn morning!"

It probably sounded like a squeak, because through the peephole, I saw a smirk creep across the doorknocker's face. "Is Beth in there?" he snarled.

I was toast.

I should have listened to my mother's lectures about the many wiles and guiles of clever girls who set out to trap a guy. Oh Lord, I should have paid attention to that little voice way way back in my head saying, "Beeeeee careful . . . you don't really know her. Man oh man, I shouldn't have drunk that tequila."

What was I to do? I went back to the bedroom and said to Beth, "There is a badass-looking guy on the landing. He's about as big as a house and he is looking for you. I don't think he is real happy. Who the hell is he?"

She pulled on her jeans and t-shirt and said, "Oh, that's Ralph. He's just a friend. Don't worry."

Yeah, sure; try not to worry when it looks like the entire local chapter of the Outlaws is prepared to break your door down in the middle of the night

"What does he want?" I hissed.

She didn't answer, but she went to the door and opened it. Just like that. She had sort of morphed into a little harder edged, colder personality since the door banging began. I was starting to figure I might have missed a few clues as to whom this cute girl really was. She stepped out of the open door and shut it behind her. Ralph? Just a friend? He was huge and looked like he just did a dime in the big house.

While she was outside having a little chat with Ralph and his posse, I was thinking that my life might be spared if I can somehow make it look like Beth had just gotten there. I went to my room, made the bed, turned on the TV, and disposed of as much party evidence as I possibly could. I unscrewed the handle out of a mop, leaned it against the wall, and sat down at the table, waiting for the attack I feared was coming.

She was outside for a good thirty minutes. They raised their voices, but not in blood-curdling screams, so my mood began to get a little hopeful.

When the door opened, I stood up, ready to grab the mop handle and at least go to my grave swinging. She stood inside the doorway, and no one barged past her, intent on tearing me to pieces. No one was at the door and no one was on the landing. Whoever they were, they were gone.

She came in and sat down at the kitchen table, a place where only a few hours before she had been a mesmerizing, dark-haired beauty with an exotic background. Now, in the harsh overhead glare of sudden reality, she looked more like five miles of bad road. She turned on the faucet and the tears began to flow. I was relieved to not be on my way to the morgue, but I was also curious about what she was into and with what I had gotten myself involved.

She cried some more and said, "Mark, you don't need to know any of this. I'm sorry I got you into it. You seem like a nice guy. You didn't do anything wrong. Could you take me somewhere?"

Although I wasn't feeling as attracted to her as I had been earlier, I have always been a sucker for a damsel in distress, so I felt my foolish mouth open and heard myself say, "Where to?"

Damn, guys can be dumb.

We piled into my faithful Pinto and headed into Florence. I followed her directions into town. She claimed all we were doing was taking her to another friend's house where she could crash for the rest of the night.

"That friend's name wouldn't happen to be Ralph, would it?" I asked.

"No, this is my best girlfriend's house, and I stay with her sometimes," she said with a sigh.

This doesn't feel right, but I am too damn tired now, and maybe I can just drop her off and never see her again, I thought.

Twenty minutes later, we pull into the driveway of what appears to be a vacant house in an upper class neighborhood.

"Are you sure we're at the right house?" I asked.

"Yeah, yeah, just turn off the lights. We need to wait a minute."

I hit the switch as darkness fell upon us, and the sound of a distant dog barking enveloped us. We sat there for a good thirty minutes and no girlfriend comes.

"We gotta go," she said. "They, uh, I mean 'she' isn't coming."

She started crying again and, against my better judgment, I said, "I have a 9 a.m. class in the morning. I can't just put you out on the highway. Let's go back to my apartment, and you can just get a cab to wherever it is you need to go in the morning."

She slid down in her seat and said, "Okay."

The next day I left my apartment and made it to class on time, but I was very fatigued. Beth called a taxi before I left and, although worn out from a long night, I was thrilled she left

Phew!

I managed to find the ever-elusive campus parking space, one that was at least closer than two miles from my classroom, anyway. Switching off the ignition, I gathered my books and stepped out of the car.

Just as I pushed the lock down, swung the door shut, and started to walk toward the classroom building, I hear, "Mr. Herndon?"

I turn and there are two guys in suits wearing a badge on their belts.

"Would you mind if we asked you a few questions?" they asked, advancing on me and holding up their police IDs.

My first thought was Ralph.

"Sure," I said. "I've got class, though."

"Well, Mr. Herndon, I'm glad you think your time is so special, but you are in a lot of trouble, young man," he said.

I remember the "right to remain silent" drill. I remember the handcuffs. I remember the ride to the police station, thinking I wished Ralph had come into the apartment and cut me down. I remember a long interrogation session under some very bright lights.

I was never charged with anything. Perhaps they were just putting on a show, trying to get me to cave, thinking I was part of who they were really after. Luckily, I was never booked, so there is no criminal record. I was just in the wrong place at the wrong time.

Several days later, I came to find out that they had picked up Beth when she got out of the taxi at the train station. She and Ralph were fugitives and were part of an interstate car-theft ring. Ralph was also wanted on accessory to murder charges in another state. The gang that showed up at my apartment was Beth's employer. She would befriend unsuspecting people—like me—gain access to their dwellings, and make off with their vehicles shortly thereafter. Why she never took mine, I will never know. The house we went to that night was a place where she and her friends would meet to get their orders from a higher-up in the gang. The cops had it staked out for a time before we got there that night. They ran my plates and followed me.

I compartmentalized and pushed that episode to the back of my head by working even harder at pursuing my music dreams. Thinking I could be called upon at any moment to join the next band bound for rock n' roll immortality, the last thing I wanted was to be saddled with a girlfriend. For some strange reason, I just wasn't that interested in chasing love, after the proverbial first time scored me a brush with organized crime and the law.

Jeeee-zus! I couldn't imagine how I would handle it if I was ever part of a band and had women throwing themselves at me all the time.

CHAPTER 12

Big Daddy

I dropped out of college in 1977. I was bitten pretty good by the music bug by then, and not much else mattered to me.

During my last semester, I had enrolled in Naval ROTC as a way to get into flight training. My big dream of becoming a fighter pilot was smashed to the ground, however. The military budget was being slashed to pieces by the Carter administration. With not many flight school slots available, they would take only applicants with perfect eyesight, of course, and a grade point average of 3.5 or higher. No waivers were granted whatsoever. I have astigmatism and, well, the GPA was languishing in the two-point-low region. So, looking at a future desk job in the service, I said, "Screw it! This college stuff is not for me." I then went to work for a landscaping company, got another apartment, and decided to pursue music in every spare moment.

The southern rock explosion was at its peak, and it captivated me. Lynyrd Skynyrd, the Allman Brothers, The Marshall Tucker Band, Charlie Daniels Band, and Atlanta Rhythm Section were in a class all by themselves. I more or less learned by playing along to their records on the set of drums in my bedroom. I set two stereo speakers on either side of my head, and I put a turntable on a piece of plywood hung from the ceiling so the needle wouldn't skip from the vibrations filing the room from the drums. On off days, I would spend seven or eight hours at a time practicing that way.

My neighbors were mostly college kids from Francis Marion where I had recently attended. Like I said—mostly. I came to blows with a guy who wasn't a student one evening. We went at it pretty good for a while until somebody called the cops. The fight broke up before the law got there. Neither of us really won the fight, but I kept on playing and practicing and he didn't hassle me anymore.

The thing is, it really wasn't practice to me—it was me playing to the imaginary people up in the nosebleed section, playing out to a sea of faces and a forest of arms in the air, filling a sold-out arena. Sometimes a whole day would be gone in what seemed like thirty minutes.

My poor angry neighbor might have been banging on the door, but I was in another world. I reckon he just gave up. To him I'd like to say, "Wherever and whoever you are now, I'm sorry for being a pecker-head, but it was worth it."

After that, I began to play in a few local bands, and we even landed some local gigs. Man, did I think I was big time! I was a pro! Now mind you, the only difference between a pro and an amateur is that the pro gets paid. I even got a taste of how ugly the biz can be, too.

One of the bands I played in for a while was a rock group called Magic City. We got a gig playing at a hole-in-the-wall club called Big Daddy's Lounge in Latta, South Carolina.

Back then, Latta was a one caution-light speed trap with a smattering of mom-and-pop stores and a few trailers scattered around, about twenty miles south of Florence. I think the club was a tobacco barn before it was a watering hole, because the atmosphere was unfinished, to say the least.

During daytime, the place was dark as a tomb. The floor was packed dirt. One stinky gas heater squatted in the center of the room, it's blue flames hissing and throwing off just enough warmth to heat the space where two or three old frazzled stuffed chairs sat amidst peanut hulls, cigarette butts, and empty beer cans. Depending on the season, the rest of the room shivered or sweltered. It was surrounded by walls covered by only the patchy siding—no insulation, no drywall, just boards with drafty space between them. I reckon building codes did not apply to places like that back then. Someone had thrown together a bar made of ply-wood with a cash register on top.

This is where ole Big Daddy himself sat all night, taking in money for beer, wine, and God knows what else. The stage, on the opposite side of the room, was constructed of wooden pallets held together by a big musty piece of carpet some-one had nailed down.

The bathroom was missing most of the outside wall where one of the urinals once hung. A small sink clung to the other wall, mostly brown from the minerals in the water—I hope. If you had any other business in there besides peeing, you could step through the gaping hole in the wall and visit the outhouse standing a few steps into the piney woods out back.

We were thrilled because we had been booked to play there every night for a week, which equaled one hundred and twenty-five bucks! Boy, were we getting somewhere now. Actually, as I remember it, despite the ghastly condition of the place, things went pretty well. We showed up on time, played four sets each night, and people got drunk and danced and swung a few fists. That was status quo in a place like that.

On Saturday night, when we finished packing up our stuff, Big Daddy wasn't there at the cash register to pay us. "Y'all come back on Monday and he'll have your money," was all we were told.

After work on Monday, we went down there and Big Daddy said he didn't do as well as he had thought, but he would pay us on Wednesday. Well, you guessed it, Wednesday came and no money.

This went on for several more days, with the excuses getting more pitiful each time, and Big Daddy's irritation growing worse along with them. He was called Big Daddy for a reason. This guy was massive; he must have stood six-foot-six and weighed over three hundred pounds, none of it fatty tissue. To me, he looked more like a wall than a man, always dressed in overalls, usually with no shirt underneath, even in the cold. He had black shoulder-length hair and a permanent scowl on his face hidden mostly by a thick beard that went down his chest. Big Daddy looked every bit a mountain man stuck in the low country of South Carolina.

We let a few days go by, hoping that would resolve his financial problems, and went back down there to collect. In hindsight, we probably should have stayed home. We walked in, and as the rickety door creaked to a close behind us, Big Daddy started cussing a streak that would have made a call girl blush.

As usual, there he sat behind his cash register. "Come over here, you little hippy son-of-a-bitches," he barked. We approached him, still naïvely thinking somehow we were going to get paid. He leaned over the register and appeared to swell in size. "I told you, dammit; I ain't got the money. I still ain't got it and if you come back in here again, you'll get paid with this!" Quick as lightning, he reached back behind him and jerked a double-barrel shotgun up and pointed it right in my face.

All I remember after that was backing away—my stomach turned to ice—holding my hands up, and mumbling something about being sorry. There is a faint recollection of gravel flying in a parking lot, tires squealing on pavement, and a fast ride back to Florence, but not much else.

To this day, every time I hear "Gimme Three Steps," I think of Big Daddy's Lounge and how I was still not yet a pro.

CHAPTER 13

Thunderbird Beginning

A great bird whose beating wings
Make the thunder and stir the wind

Lakota Sioux Legend

*   *   *

The first professional gig came along not long after the Big Daddy debacle. An opening came with a top-40 variety band that had steady gigs every weekend.

The bandleader was a local legend around Florence. To say the man was unique would be an understatement. Ed Turbeville had been a fixture on the local music scene thirty years prior to me coming on board. He had played with some of the great swing bands of the 1940s. He was old-school hard-ass. He liked me, but he ruled his band with an iron fist. I didn't like his approach at first, but I came to respect him. His admonishments to me on all the little nuances about looking professional were sage advice that unfortunately took me about thirty years to apply to myself.

I remember one thing in particular he said to me one night not long after I started with him. We were playing at the Elks Lodge in Florence. He found me in the back, sitting at the bar, nursing a scotch before we were to start the first set.

He shook his head, saying, "Maaahk, if you can't do it straight, you can't do it at all."

Looking back at everything I have been lucky enough to live through, I can't begin to describe just how profound that was. I wish I had not been so hard-headed back then, but who isn't when you're twenty-two?

We played current top-40 stuff and old standards. We were an eight-piece band that featured a beautiful, classy African-American female singer named Sally. She was my best friend in the band, and I thought the world of her. We had the traditional bandstand set-up with the horns. They had little podiums in front of them holding their sheet music, and when it came time to play their parts, each player would stand up. Ed conducted while playing stand-up and electric bass, depending on the tune. Except for Sally, we all wore wine-red jackets with tux shirts and bowties underneath. Here I was, the next rock-and-roll legend waiting in the wings to be discovered, but I had to dress like a waiter to go play. Oh well, we do what we have to do.

Ed was about sixty-five years old when I started with him. He stood, or stooped, only about five feet tall. He couldn't help that, of course, but it still struck me as funny when he would stand next to his upright bass. Turning around to growl at me about playing something sloppy, he would remind me of a troll under a bridge, holding an oversized fiddle. He had jet-black-dyed hair, dark eyes, and an equally jet-black-dyed mustache. He combed his hair back in the style of the gangster era and always wore a little stage make-up. He looked like Don Corleone played by Marlon Brando from the *Godfather* movie. Behind all the gruff, he was a really good man.

In order to save me gas, he would always ask me to ride with him in the Batmobile to gigs. He kept it stocked with drinks and snacks, sometimes sandwiches his sweet wife, Mary, would make for us. The Batmobile was a 1966 stretch Cadillac limousine with long fins, a little hail damage in places, and some spotty decorative oxidation on all the chrome. I think he had purchased it from a funeral home years before. Nonetheless, he was proud of it. It had a vibe to it. It was black with blacked-out windows before that look was in style. He had a hitch made onto the back of the car that pulled an equally black trailer emblazoned with "Ed Turbeville and His Orchestra" in big bright green-and-white letters. It got attention, to say the least.

The guy would drive all night sometimes getting to and from gigs, and then want to party till sunrise after we got home. He would keep me wide-awake driving back with hysterical tales of the vaudeville and swing-band era. Phew! I don't know where he got his energy, but I used think it was from a little more than Geritol.

Sally and I became close through sharing experiences on the road with Ed. She was my soulmate although we were never romantically involved. Ed ruled with an iron fist, and it could get discouraging from time to time. She always provided pep talks when things like an ass-chewing from Ed would get me down. Sally had been working for Ed several years before I came along, so she knew how to take him with a grain of salt. At one point, she had been a national touring act signed to a major label, so I took what she would say to heart. I was new to professional gigs then, and didn't have the thick skin it requires to withstand the criticism.

With time and experience one learns to either roll with it and apply parts of it constructively, or to find something else to do. I hung in there and didn't quit, many times because of Sally's encouragement. I listened to her because she had a lot of stories of survival herself. In the 1960s and '70s in South Carolina, it wasn't always easy for a black female to rise above the status in which she was raised.

She did, and she did it without ever holding a grudge or blaming anyone for holding her back. She believed in herself as a person, and she reached a lot of goals by doing just that.

On the long drives back home from gigs, we would philosophize about various things, riding through the night. We would fantasize about all the cool things either of us would do if one of us were to ever really make it.

She had a hysterical sense of humor, and some nights when Ed was prattling away with a story, I would listen instead to her tell some damn good stories of her own. She would revert back to ghetto-speak and have me rolled up on the floor laughing. It got even funnier when Ed would think we were laughing at his stories from up front.

I have lost touch with Sally over the years, but I will never forget her, my first soulmate on the road. Wherever you are, Sally, my friend, I hope it's in a spotlight on a stage somewhere.

Of course now, with a few years and a few million miles of my own behind me, I realize Ed was someone who just truly loved what he did. I had a pretty good day job in Florence, and I was playing music every weekend with Ed. He and his wife were good people. They really became my family.

Not a bad lot in life right?

Not at all, but my spirit was restless for more. I craved the life I imagined far away, out on the road, so I was always networking to find a gig that would take me there. I found it in the last place I ever would have looked.

My mother now worked as front desk manager at the Thunderbird Motor Inn there in town. With her show-business background, she always knew how to make the musicians a little more at home while playing the nightclub there. She knew how to talk and listen to the many road people who would pass through. I can tell you from experience, that is rare for a touring musician and so much appreciated when it happens. We are patronized and stereotyped too often.

Being a good mom, too, my mother always had her ear tuned to any talk of these traveling bands needing a drummer.

In late 1978 there was such a group, a band consisting of three cousins from a small town in Alabama. When hearing that their present drummer had given notice, she discreetly told me to just come hear them and hang out at the club, maybe try to score an audition. She never once said anything to them about "my son this or my son that." Pretty cool.

Well, I went and checked them out, talked to them a little on one of their breaks, and managed to arrange for an audition the next day.

I showed up at one of the rooms and we began talking about my musical background and influences, etc.

Just about the time we were going to head down to the bar to play a little and see if I could hack it, the phone rang in the room. The lead singer answered it. I could only hear one side of the conversation, but it went like this: "Hello? Yes, this is he ... Ughh ... no, we're not busy, what can we do for you? Ughh ... Ugh ... Ughh ... I see ... Hmmn ... we might be able to have it all out of there by four. Okay ... All right then, we'll be down in a few minutes. Well, I'm sorry, too. Bye."

I knew what had happened. The band had just been fired. The bar manager had fired them only because they didn't play enough disco. They played everything from Roy Acuff to ZZ Top, but not enough disco.

Disco put a lot of good bands out of business then, just like karaoke does now. *Ugh!* In those days the silk-shirted, leisure-suited clientele that dug the disco scene drank liquor more than anything else. The bar manager really liked the band, but they brought in the beer drinking, blue-collar crowd. In the bar business you make your profit on liquor, not beer. Simple economics. The band had to be replaced.

It was awkward in that motel room, to say the least.

I gave everybody my phone number and said, "Well, maybe another time, blah, blah, blah. Take care, guys, blah, blah, blah. Good luck, man, blah, blah, blah," and so on. With that I hurried for the stairs and drove off in my car thinking, *Jeez! Glad I didn't get that gig. Those guys can't even keep one!*

It was October 1978. Besides working my day job driving a delivery truck, and playing for Ed Turbeville, I was working whenever possible with some other guys in Augusta, Georgia, trying to put together a rock band down there. We played some gigs, but there were some internal problems from the get-go. Some frustrating time went by, and the inevitable day came to throw in the towel.

As I was packing my drums into my faithful, trusty, rusty red Pinto, the guy there who owned all the gear stuck his head out and hollered. "Hey, there's a guy from Myrtle Beach on the phone ..."

Chapter 14

The Bowery

When I answered the phone, a voice said, "Hey, man. I play with that group that got fired in Florence. Do you remember me?

It was the getting-fired part that jarred my memory, and I started to laugh out loud, but for once kept my mouth shut.

"We have a summer-long house gig at the Bowery in Myrtle Beach," he continued. "Our drummer quit and we need someone. I remember talking to you back in Florence. Are you interested?"

Was I interested? I'm not sure. Did I have anything to lose?

Nope.

"Yeah," I heard my mouth say. "When?"

"Tomorrow morning, if you can make it," he said.

Too far—I'd be way late.

"Sure, man, I'll be there!" I said.

I drove to the Myrtle Beach that night and got there about 4:30 a.m. I fell asleep in my car somewhere on Ocean Boulevard with the sound of the surf seeming to whisper, "Dri-ffFFFter . . . Dri-ffFFFter . . . FffffoolisSHHH . . . FffffoolisSHHH . . . Dri-fFFFter."

The next morning at about 9:30 I parked in front of the Bowery and waited.

They showed up about fifteen minutes later at 9:45. I liked that. Maybe this might be something after all.

"What do you want to play?" asked the bass player once we got set up.

"I don't know—anything, I reckon," I said. "I've been playing with a Top-40 cover band lately, so anything current, I guess.

"He thought for a moment and said, "How 'bout, 'Play That Funky Music (White Boy)'?"

"Sure." I counted it off and we hit that sweet spot immediately.

We then played three or four other tunes popular at the time. Everything seemed to fit together really well, and I noticed right off how good the singing was.

"Man, you guys have vocals like the Eagles," I said.

"Well, we grew up singing together; we ought to sound like *somebody* by now," the lead guitar player quipped.

A short time later, the lead singer, who appeared to be in charge of the outfit, pulled me aside and we walked down to the boardwalk overlooking the Atlantic Ocean. It was mid-March 1979. Seagulls were wheeling overhead; the light breeze was rustling the palm trees, stirring the spring-fresh ocean air into my nose.

There was not a cloud in the sky, the sun was shining brightly, and the light was shimmering off the azure-blue water, bringing everything into sharp focus. He and I sat on the stairs, having a chuckle about what had happened in Florence. I remember he asked me what I wanted to do in music.

Remembering my "pact" with the Carolina Coliseum, I said, "Above all, someday I want to play concerts to sold-out houses. I don't really think or care about much else right now."

"That's cool, man. Are you married or got anything keeping you close to home?" he asked.

"Nope, I'm free," I said.

We sat there not saying much for the next few minutes, just sort of soaking up the vibe.

Then he got up and said, "I need to go talk to the others."

I learned sometime later that it wasn't my very average playing ability at the time that got me in, it was my desire to go all the way, at all costs, and being ready and willing to do so. It was also about the fact that I had showed up on time for the audition. I guess that impressed the three guys because many of the other drummers stood them up before and, understandably, punctuality was of upmost importance to them. I was delighted to have found like-minded people who were really serious about making it.

I served out my two weeks' notice with Ed in Florence and moved to Myrtle Beach, South Carolina. I started full time, six nights a week, playing at the Bowery on April Fool's Day 1979. I made two-hundred dollars cash each week and didn't have a day job. I was a real musician—a pro at last.

The Bowery had a somewhat notorious reputation in Myrtle Beach. To say it was a dive then would be gross understatement. It was a step up from Big Daddy's, but not a big one. But, at least the bathrooms were enclosed. It was located in an alleyway about a hundred feet back from the waterfront.

The city used the alley to store its trash dumpsters. Located across from it stairs led up to the back of the Myrtle Beach Pavilion, where occasional nationally touring bands would play upstairs.

At night it was dark in the alley. The police would park the paddy wagon in front of the Bowery to haul away the bums, drunks, and tourists alike for just about everything you could imagine. I saw a lot of fights both inside and out.

A waiter there, Bruce, proved himself a total badass in a fight. He hit a guy so hard one night, he sent him airborne out the front door. The guy lay sprawled on the sidewalk outside with a broken jaw, his shoes still *inside* where he had been standing in them a few seconds before.

Not knowing the local laws, I stepped out the door one night with a draft beer in my hand—and got slapped with a citation for drinking in public. I had to pay right on the spot or get a ride in the paddy wagon. I think some of the cops back then resented us for the packed house we were getting during the season. Things got really bad with many people being arrested for nothing. At one point a camera crew from the TV show *60 Minutes* set up on the roof of the Bowery to expose some of the unjust harassment on tourists by the Myrtle Beach PD. It never went on air, but I think several police officers and the chief were relieved of duty. Needless to say, I furiously minded my own business.

The Bowery was a rough and raw place, dirty, with no air conditioning; but it was surrounded by all the action happening at the beach in those days. I could feel the excitement in the air most nights, riding my bike into work.

Many bars with live music lined Ocean Boulevard back then. An amusement park filled the area catty-corner across the street. The bright lights, clanking rides, noisy arcades, and loud music that spilled out onto the street created a constant carnival-like energy. It got into people. It got into me. The nightlife atmosphere was something I had always taken to, starting way back in the days of adolescent mischief. I just always felt more alive once the sun went down. Apparently, so did all of Myrtle Beach.

During the summer of 1979, I lived in an apartment only about two miles down Ocean Boulevard from the Bowery. It was a dive, just like I was accustomed to. It was really more of just a large room upstairs in an old two-story house built before World War II, converted into housing for lifeguards working for the summer.

I never locked the door because it was off its hinges. I would just kind of wedge it back into place when I left. The whole structure was off- kilter because it was gradually collapsing.

My apartment had room for a bed, one small desk, an antique refrigerator, a stove—except there was no stove, just the space where one once sat—and a very questionable-looking 220 outlet on the wall. I imagined there would be a fire soon after plugging anything into it, so I left it alone.

The entire floor slanted about five degrees downward, just enough to make things really interesting if I were to come back in during the wee hours with my walking skills a little wobbly. The bathroom had a big hole next to the commode where the floor had rotted away. Through that hole, I could look down into the house kitchen where the old couple that owned the place (Don and Bell) would cook for everybody many nights.

It sounds really unsanitary, and probably was, but when you are damn near starving, it doesn't matter. I'd jump into the shower before going into work and would holler down through the hole, "What's for supper tonight, Bell?" and she would yell back the menu.

She and her husband were great people even though the place was a wreck. In a way, they sort of looked after all my wild neighbors and me, and they kept us fed.

I could live with no AC, a slanted floor, and the hole in the bathroom, I reckon. I was happy. I was in a band—at the beach—playing every night! When you are twenty-three with no attachments or real responsibilities, you tend to overlook things like amenities.

Back then, I would always look forward to the music at night. Granted, the Bowery wasn't packed every night, but like I said, during peak season it was. I was learning a few things, too.

The guys had been doing this gig for about five summers before I came along. I replaced a drummer who was from Nashville. People liked him because he was a really good singer, or so I heard. I didn't sing. I still don't.

During the audition for the band, I opened my big mouth and said out of necessity that I had been doing a little singing in the band I was previously with.

I forget which song they were going over. The bass player promptly got a mic stand and put it back there next to the drum riser and said, "Okay, let's try it." About halfway through that tune, he came back and just took the stand back to where it was. Nobody said anything, but I got the message.

Some of the regulars and the guy who managed the Bowery at the time, "Bugs," were not my biggest fans. Maybe it was because I couldn't sing, or maybe because I put all my rock influences into what the guys were playing. I guess it was a big change for some folks used to a certain sound. I don't know, but that was what I felt like I brought to the table, and I wasn't going to let anybody change me.

The other three came under some pressure from Bugs and the regulars to get rid of me. I remember our lead singer telling them all to shove it, and that I was the damn drummer, and if they didn't like it, tough shit.

Now, that bought some loyalty from me, to say the least. I really liked that guy back then. He was the one who always seemed to be the cool head, the one on my side, pulling for me, understanding the newcomer's hardships trying to find a niche within the band and with its followers.

He and I used to play golf at a little backwater golf course on Sunday afternoons. Our golfing skills left lots to be desired, but it was fun. Another band member would join us occasionally. He would play barefooted. None of us could really afford green fees, much less fancy golf shoes.

After a couple swings with the ball either going in the water or woods, the barefoot player would get madder than hell. He would throw his clubs into the trees, and sometimes they wouldn't come down. He would beat the ground and cuss like a salty old petty officer with forty years at sea.

Once, he even threw his whole bag of clubs into the pond after a bad hit. It was hysterical for me.

We would watch these fits from a safe distance and lie on the ground, laughing our guts out. Often, a club or ball would come zinging over my head while I lay there doubled up. I would look up and he would be storming away, back toward the trailer that was the clubhouse, get in his old car, sling gravel in the air, and speed off.

He would always be fine at the gig later that night, though—even laugh about it himself. It got to where the days he didn't come were almost boring. God, it was funny.

We might not have been making real money, but it was still the best of times. We shared a sense of mission, camaraderie, and friendship. I appreciate those times so much now. Things really weren't all that bad, and they sure were simple. We had those things no amount of success can ever buy.

It was rough, but real, and it was a blessing.

CHAPTER 15

Looks Like "We" Made It

I held Aladdin's lamp . . .
Someone came and took the lamp away
I looked around, a lousy candle's all I found

"Magic Carpet Ride"
John Kay
Steppenwolf

*   *   *

Many people would come to Myrtle Beach from all over the country, hear us, buy a record from the stage, then go back and get their hometown radio stations to play it. It was nationwide promotion without ever having to leave, and it was golden. We also did a great bit of our own radio promotion. We would split up, two to a car, and drive out to stations in the area. We would beg, borrow, or steal, as the saying goes, to get them to give us a break. The local stations would, as did some of the others in the Carolina region. Yep. You could do that in those days, before there was such a thing as corporate radio. If you try that sort of thing nowadays as an indie, well, good luck.

In those times we made lifelong friends in radio, just by doing things the old way. All this radio activity, plus people going back home from their vacations and asking their local stations to play some of the band's tunes, began to get some recognition.

In 1980, the group managed to chart regionally in the Southeast with a song titled "I Wanna Come Over."

We had tremendous support from our friends in radio there. We got a lot of support outside the box from the rock station there in Myrtle Beach, WKZQ. The record was pop sounding enough to make it into their format, and they played it a lot. This regional buzz got the attention of a small record label from Dallas, Texas. They came to see us play, liked what they saw, and added us to their roster.

The first single they released was "My Home's In Alabama." It was released in the early part of 1980. By April, it had charted on the Billboard's The Hot 100 in the '70s. I still remember the night the lead singer came into the Bowery, jumping up and down in the entrance hallway, so excited that we had broken The Hot 100.

The band got the attention of some major labels in Nashville. Hence, we got the much-coveted invitation to perform on the "New Faces Show" at the Country Radio Seminar held in March of that year. That show was, and still is, one of the biggest breaks any artist can get in this business.

I was suddenly in Nashville with only one summer at the Bowery under my belt and the winter month's spent scratching a meager existence playing in a series of dingy roadside bars with this band. We were here to perform for all the big labels in town. They, along with the who's-who of the broadcast industry, were there to see and hear the up-and-comers.

There was a little buzz going around about us, but most people had never heard us live. At this oh-so-important show, labels are able to get a sample of new talent to possibly sign and the radio folks get a peek at who to watch so they can claim being first to break a hot new artist in their respective markets.

Sometimes, those new artists get to be big. I remember the band shared the stage that night with another unknown, a little redheaded pistol of a female singer from Oklahoma named Reba.

It was a high-pressure gig, and not for the faint-hearted, to say the least, but "we" were ready. I say "we" because we weren't all part of it. It got really weird, and probably should have gotten more of my attention than it did, when we found out the show's organizers had already hired a backup band to play all the artists' material, including ours.

Larry McBride, the head of the minor label, MDJ Records, which we were on at the time, said "Mark, man, I know this is strange, but you won't be on stage for the show tonight. It's only going to be the other three, and they only get to sing."

"Huh, what?" I asked.

"Yeah," Larry continued. "We tried to get you up there with the guys, but the people running this thing said 'no,' this is the way things are done in Nashville. They ain't never had a band on one of these shows, so they don't know what to do with y'all."

I was very disappointed coming from a rock background thinking that a band is a band no matter what. "Are you sure?" I asked.

"Yeah, we ain't real happy with it, but I don't want to make waves right now. These musicians are really good session players and can read the charts for all the music."

One of the tunes in our set for that night, "My Home's In Alabama," had a rather complicated Southern Rock-influenced arrangement to it, and I was skeptical. "Uh oh," was all I could say, and all I could think was, *Danger! Danger, Will Robinson!*

It finally came time for the other three to take the stage. The performance area was dimly lit under a low-hanging ceiling in one of the ballrooms of the Hyatt Regency. "Stage production" was a small P.A. system and a foldout platform like they use for luncheon speakers to address the Rotary Club.

A set of drums sat in the center with instruments, amps, and wires everywhere. The players were busy shuffling their charts under the little lights on their music stands. The room was almost claustrophobic, packed with people and overflowing with the buzz of loud conversation. I was probably more nervous standing out in the crowd, feeling like a fish out of water, than the other three must have been, about to perform.

Here's my band at a giant crossroads, and I can't play with them. This performance could be the night that decides whether dreams come true, or we go back to slogging it out in dark smoky bars, not much better that Big Daddy's, where nobody gives a damn about you or your music. Forever! I didn't do much praying in those days, but I did that night.

Those prayers were answered; the guys pulled it off somehow, and the rest, as they say, is history. Reba, obviously, did well, too. Of course, now I can see how naïve I was back then.

The band was signed to a long-term contract with RCA Records soon after the show. I heard that "we" got signed about a week later. I was not invited to that meeting, whenever or wherever it took place. From that milestone night onward, something changed. I was not then, or ever, to be officially included with the rest of the band as far as any dealings where the record company was concerned.

Oddly enough, it seems this decree did not come from the record company, but from the others in the band, for reasons that I never want to understand.

It was then that I became a salaried contract employee.

Our faithful bird for 11 years—
good ole "Twelve Oh Eight Alabama"

My newlywed mom and dad just before he shipped
out to the Pacific (September 1943)

Me and Dad (Christmas 1955)

Colonel John L. Herndon, commanding officer,
Marine Aircraft Groups 24, MCAS Cherry Point, NC (1967)

*Mother, always the life of the party, in HER element,
a house full of laughter and cheers*

*Dad, far right, in HIS element as I will always remember him with his
fellow Marines and pilots. Da Nang, South Vietnam (1968)*

...and 50 years later

Never underestimate a geek!
(Senior year at Camden Military)

Graduation was a miracle for both me and my parents.

*Me (far left) in front of my ragtag "Platoon B" during
Graduation Day Parade (May 1974)*

With Sally and Mary after the show in Myrtle Beach some 25 years after I had played and toured with Ed Turbeville

Not long out of the Bowery, we still had a long way to go, but didn't know it. Note the plywood and low-hanging lights.
(Circa 1984)

*Tearing up the York Fair in York, PA. This was the show where we
gambled so much and came close to paying the ultimate price
later on in a fuel-starved jet.*

*Not EVERYONE was impressed with us—
especially not with me!*

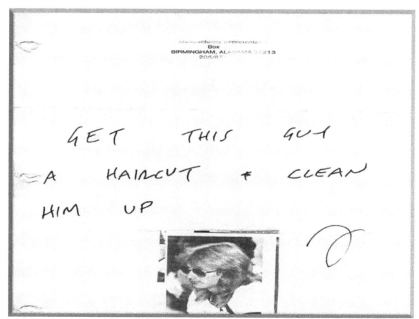

Another note from a concerned fan

Would you trust these two hooligans to fly you anywhere?

*Just before launch in the Blue Angels' "Seven Jet", a TA-4F.
I can't believe it wasn't a dream.*

*Throughout the years with the band, I managed to score some great stick
time in some amazing airplanes. This, the F-15E, was probably the finest.
I couldn't resist the "hero pose" after the flight.*

THIS is why we did it . . .

*One of the things I will always miss the most . . . the buzz of
anticipation from the crowd right before the house lights go out.
This picture was an ad in* Billboard Magazine
for the week of CMA. (Circa 1986)

Me, Ron Wood of the Rolling Stones, and Billy Idol at Elaine's in NYC (Fall 1983). I always wanted country and rock to mingle more, long before Crossroads.

Me... Cocky?

Nah… Never…

USS ALABAMA (SSBN 731)
COMMISSIONING
25 MAY 1985

TO MR. MARK HERNDON
IN APPRECIATION FOR YOUR STRONG SUPPORT

A great honor… I got to be the guy to send her down the rails with the champagne bottle burst. I wonder if that gold record I sent the crew afterward still hangs in their dining room.

Perception...

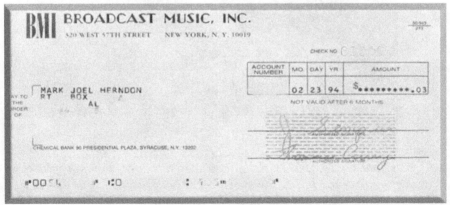

A check for 3 cents... Reality!

Me and the guys with Charlie Daniels and Charlie Hayward (his long-time bassist during our 2½ years of touring together).
Charlie Daniels will always be one of my heroes.

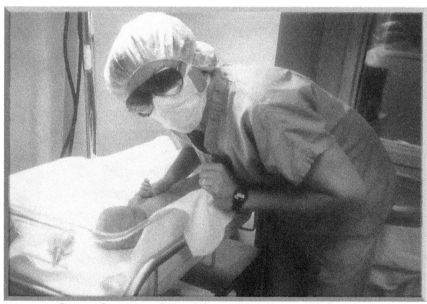

Game changer... Me with my 10-minute-old daughter,
Katie Michelle Herndon (February 20, 1989)

I finally had someone my own age to play with...

...Who grew into my traveling pal and soulmate...

. . . Who I wound up having to give away.
(Proudly, though; and I gained a great son-in-law as a bonus.)

From a beat-up '70s Dodge van with some drums and amps thrown in the back and four determined young guys... to all of this. I never got tired of standing out here, listening to all that power at idle.

Carolina Coliseum, Columbia, S.C., the night of "I told ya so . . ."

...And 26 years later in Birmingham. Notice the lighters held high?
It never died, not in my heart anyway.

The President and Mrs. Reagan
request the pleasure of your company
at a reception to be held at
The White House
on Tuesday afternoon, March 15, 1983
at five o'clock

Enter Southwest Gate

Proud to say, I met the man. Nobody's filled those shoes since.

*A good way to draw the final curtain, my induction into
the Country Music Hall of Fame (November 15, 2005)*

My first civilian job after the "Farewell Tour."
It felt so good to be back in aviation full-time.
I swore I would never pick up a drumstick again.
(You know what they say about the word "never.")

They say nothing's set in stone . . .

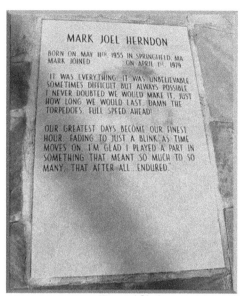

MARK JOEL HERNDON

BORN ON MAY 11ᵀᴴ 1955 IN SPRINGFIELD, MA
MARK JOINED   ON APRIL 1ˢᵀ 1979

IT WAS EVERYTHING. IT WAS UNBELIEVABLE,
SOMETIMES DIFFICULT BUT ALWAYS POSSIBLE
I NEVER DOUBTED WE WOULD MAKE IT, JUST
HOW LONG WE WOULD LAST. DAMN THE
TORPEDOES, FULL SPEED AHEAD!

OUR GREATEST DAYS BECOME OUR FINEST
HOUR, FADING TO JUST A BLINK AS TIME
MOVES ON. I'M GLAD I PLAYED A PART IN
SOMETHING THAT MEANT SO MUCH TO SO
MANY, THAT AFTER ALL, ENDURED.

. . . Even if it is.

CHAPTER 16

Playin' the Odds

Eternal Father, lend Thy grace
To those with wings who fly thro' space,
Thro' wind and storm, thro' sun and rain,
Oh bring them safely home again.
Oh Father, hear a humble prayer,
For those in peril in the air!

From "The Navy Hymn"

*   *   *

We went back to playing the Bowery while the record company began to make plans for introducing their newest acquisition to the world. We would stay there until July of that summer.

We played a farewell concert at the Myrtle Beach Convention Center on July 4th. It was sold out. The headliner was supposed to be Jimmy Buffet, an up-and-coming artist. The news of the boys down at the Bowery getting signed to RCA was all over the beach by now. Everyone turned out to see us off—the boys who had made it.

Jimmy came into the dressing room with a case of Budweiser for us tucked under his arm. "Man, you guys need to close the show. This is your crowd. They came to see you. If I try and close it, I may not make it out of here alive." Wow. Pretty big of him, I thought, but smart, too. Myrtle Beach did, in fact, turn out to see us.

The room was standing-room-only, and I think there might have been a riot if Mr. Buffet had not been so wise. Like the people there, I too might have gone to see a band who never in their lives had done much more than scratch out a pittance playing dive bars and selling a few t-shirts and records, much less go from there to arena headliner in one day. As a spectator, I might have gone for the excitement of seeing a hometown band that had the raw beginnings of the right stuff and were on their way to bigger things. I believe we did, because somehow, even with our lack of experience in an arena setting, we held the room till the last song. We played two encores with the crowd standing in their seats and no one leaving to beat the traffic.

When it was over, I don't think any of us were on this Earth for at least three days. We had no idea that what lay ahead was not going to be anything like that night's flirt with the future. Suddenly, it seemed the world lay at our feet. The start of a new life loomed large and boundless.

It was the start of a new decade, too. We had a new president: Ronald Reagan. Millions tuned in on the TV to find out who shot J.R., then tuned in again to see who shot John Lennon. Gas was one dollar and nineteen cents, and Mt. Saint Helens blew up.

Leaving Myrtle Beach, we started traveling a lot. Shows were still mostly clubs and a smattering of opening-act gigs. In those days, the band on stage was only the four of us. We had a high-energy, kick-ass live show. Many times we would get an encore when opening for a major name artist. We knew we were doing something right. Sometimes we worried about upstaging the headliner because there was a risk of getting blackballed in the higher circles, thus not being asked to open for anyone after a point. That happened to Mother's Finest a few years before. Fortunately, that never happened. Maybe it would have, but our time in the opening-act category didn't last long enough for us to do any real damage.

That first year, we had been booked into a series of clubs down in Texas by a very savvy promoter who saw how quickly the band was becoming popular. He locked us in for about fifteen club dates for a price that, at the time, seemed like good money, but would be nothing compared to what the band would be able to ask based on the draw. Savvy, like I said. We started to get offers to come and play one-nighters at what we would normally get for a whole week. Instead, we made good on the Texas club contract. This was a very smart decision. It started to build a good reputation with promoters simply because we didn't leave one holding the bag, so to speak. The band did did take one offer, though, while honoring our obligation to the Texas promoter. It almost killed us.

An empty slot came up for an opening act on a Willie Nelson show at the Pennsylvania State Fair in York, Pennsylvania. The iconic fair promoter, George Moffett, called us. We knew who he was, so we were floored that someone that big would be calling us. We had a gig for that same night in Tyler, Texas. It was an outdoor event with a covered stage. Tyler is a college town, so it was sold out. What a bind. We were going to miss a great opportunity. Well, old George really wanted us to come and play, so he hired a private jet to pick us up and fly us to York. We would play the opening slot and, with the time-zone change gaining us one hour, be back in time to close our show in Tyler. I reckon ethics only go so far.

We hopped on that plane quick. The show in Pennsylvania went off great. I think we came back for two encores there. We got back on the plane sweaty and out of breath, ready to go back to Texas to rock some socks off. Not long after we reached cruising altitude, I went up front to bug the pilots. I was still flying in my spare time, working on building hours, hoping to advance through the ratings. I chatted with them for most of the way, probably asking way too many questions.

Almost two hours into the flight, the first officer looked back at me. "We might have a little problem," he said.

"Like what?" I asked.

"Don't think we are going to have enough fuel to make it non-stop." Whoever chartered that plane had to do it at the last minute, and probably didn't know it was the wrong one for the job. It was a 1970s model Cessna Citation I. By today's standards, it hardly qualifies as a real jet. It was designed for short hops, mainly. Pilots jokingly refer to it as the only jet in the world that comes with screens placed over the back of the engines to prevent bird strikes from the rear. It's really slow—about three-hundred-twenty knots on a good day. Add a one-hundred-fifty knot headwind and you are blistering across the ground at a whopping one-hundred-seventy knots.

Showtime came and went.

We were still airborne, fighting the wind, with a good way left to go. Back then, charter flying was not nearly as sophisticated as it is now. The only people who had data-link communication and in-flight phones were the military and some of the major airlines.

"Are we going to be late?" I asked.

"Very," the first officer said. He got on the radio and called a nearby fixed-base operator who agreed to make a call to the Tyler promoter. The promoter was going to make an announcement over the PA at the venue, telling everyone that we were in the air, running a little late, but coming as fast as we could.

He did and sent back the message, "Hurry! The crowd is getting a little restless." An understatement, to say the least.

We went on a little farther, the pilots electing to stay at high altitude longer than necessary in order to conserve fuel. It was a wash, though, considering the high wind. We felt a lot of pressure to make that gig because we were obligated—contract-wise, fan-wise, and most importantly, word-wise. The Texas promoter had agreed to let us go up to Pennsylvania based on our guarantee of making it back in time.

The flight crew decided to press on without a fuel stop. As they began the descent, I could tell the two pilots were not real happy.

"Fuel's gonna be mighty tight," they said.

I went back to my seat.

To stack the odds against us, Mother Nature brought the weather down to bare minimums at the airport. It was starting to mist and where there's mist, there's usually fog. That night it was thick in Tyler.

By the sound of the engines, I could tell we were on approach to landing, but I could see nothing outside but blackness. I knew we must be getting close to the ground because it seemed like we had been on the approach forever.

I looked out the window and saw a blue glow streak by. *That would be a taxiway light . . . Holy Crap!* I thought.

We were very low and still in the blind. I heard the engines spool up as the pilot poured the coals on to go around. The first officer said it was a missed approach and we *had* to go to the alternate field. It was about thirty miles away. I didn't know much about that level of aviation then, but I did know airplanes don't fly very far out of gas.

We started the approach at the alternate. Same thing. Down to the weeds, see nothing and go around. We were now literally on a wing and a prayer.

The crew had only two options left: either make it or crash.

I don't know how the others were feeling, but I was frightened. I was thinking we might soon be on a higher stage, jamming with Buddy Holly or the guys from Lynyrd Skynyrd in a few minutes.

Down into the breach we all went again.

We bucked through the bumps and fog, hoping for the best, bracing for the first impact.

Lady Luck or, better, Providence, smiled upon us that night. I was stretching my neck from my seat, expecting to see a Texas Longhorn steer come smashing through the windshield, when the pilot chopped the throttles about the same time as wheels hit pavement.

We made it!

We rolled out the remaining length of the runway, turned onto the taxiway, went about a hundred yards, and just like long ago on a taxiway in Cheraw, South Carolina, the right engine flamed out.

We survived the ensuing wild police escort ride to the gig—two hours late— then went straight to the stage and played our asses off. Those crazy, but loyal college kids had stayed put, waiting for us. They had been kept informed, and they seemed to understand. Somehow it made for an even better show than if things had been on schedule.

That's the way our fans were. How we got there is how things happen many times when entertainers are just trying to get from show to show. The show must go on. You do what you have to do.

The gamble paid off. We were asked to come back to the Pennsylvania State Fair many years in a row thereafter. George Moffett would also book us time and time again for hundreds of state and county fairs all over the country.

CHAPTER 17

Curses

Not long after the Tyler fiasco on the chartered jet, we found ourselves in Fallon, Nevada, for a county fair show as the headliner. We were now going from show to show on a leased bus. We had recently acquired a bus from the Marshall Tucker Band, who sold it to us to get a better one, but it was undergoing some refurbishments and would not be ready for another few weeks. The lease bus was a sorry affair, only one axle in the back, not very well air-conditioned, noisy and underpowered. But at least it was a bus.

We had ridden in much worse.

Our routing had taken us down through Nevada, across the famous White Sands Proving Ground the night before. I sat up front with the driver late that night, marveling at the snow-white sand gleaming in the moonlight. It stretched away from us, undulating underneath the scrub brush and tumbleweeds, out to the dark rocky hills defining the horizon. The air felt very warm, so the appearance of what looked like snow on either side of the highway conflicted pleasantly. I was new to sights like these and wanted to soak everything in. I spent some time thinking about the history here, where the first atomic bomb was developed and detonated in total secrecy during World War II. For the sake of the country, folks in those days kept their mouths shut.

The next morning, I awoke, sweltering in my bunk, to what sounded like crying outside the bus, which sat in the motel parking lot. I got up to investigate. I looked out to where the crying was coming from and saw a very leathery, brown-skinned old woman holding an amulet with smoke coming out of it.

Short and stooped, she wore traditional Indian buckskin clothing, adorned with handmade jewelry, featuring various bones and teeth from animals hanging from her neck. I hoped the jewelry came from animals, anyway.

Curious, I opened the door and stepped into the bright desert sunshine and oven-like heat.

She ignored me and kept on with her crying. It wasn't crying, actually, but some sort of a very eerie-sounding chant spoken in a language I had never heard—or even anything like it. She would repeat the phrase over and over while shaking the amulet toward the bus, fanning smoke against the side. She made a couple of loops around the bus, stopped, and stared at me with dark onyxes for eyes set deeply into sun-baked folds and wrinkles of skin.

"Uh, good morning," I said. "Is there something I can help you with?"

She shook her head and spoke in heavily accented Native American English. "No. This bus has been in the way of communicating with my son. He is in jail across the way, and your bus is blocking our view of each other."

I turned in the direction she pointed her bony, crooked finger and saw the slit-windowed concrete façade of the city jail about a hundred and fifty yards away, across the parking lot, shimmering in the heat waves rising off the pavement.

"What is it you are doing with the smoke and stuff?" I asked.

"Because of this bus, I am very upset. I have placed a curse on what is in the way of me helping my son," she said.

The bus driver was fast asleep in his motel room from driving all night, so I wasn't about to try and wake him because a nut job was dancing around the bus. "Okay," I said.

I went back inside and shook the blackout curtains pulled across one of the bunk spaces, waking our stage manager, Joe.

He joined me, watching her make another turn around the bus as I caught him up on what she had told me. He got a little spooked and said, "I've got some extra tickets for the show tonight. Let's give her a couple and maybe she can un-curse us."

"Sounds good to me," I said, beginning to get a little spooked myself.

I took the tickets to her. I apologized, telling her the bus could be moved later, but the driver was asleep. "Uh, I don't know much about medicine-man stuff, but could you take this curse off, by any chance? We didn't know about your son."

She shrugged and said, "I cannot do that now. Once a curse is in place it cannot ever be removed."

Figuring she was several fries short of a Happy Meal, I gave her the tickets and headed off to my motel room.

That evening in the midst of our show, with the temperatures cooling and the sun sliding low behind watchful hills, I spotted the old woman from the stage. Under a sky now the silver-blue of desert twilight, she stood in front of the stage in full Indian regalia, kicking up dust, stomping and dancing to the music we were cranking out. I watched her having a grand old time prancing around an imaginary bonfire. Security tried to get her to take her seat several times. She would have none of it, and they finally had to escort her out. She put up a fight, and it turned into a bit of a scuffle.

After that morning's encounter with her, this bugged me. Back at the hotel the next morning I decided to do something about it.

We were to leave about ten o'clock. About an hour before, I walked across the parking lot and knocked on the door of the dilapidated house that she said was being blocked from view of the city jail by our bus. I had made double sure the driver knew not to park back in the same spot after the show. It was her house. She came to the door and opened it. I told her I was sorry that she got treated badly at the show and I hoped she had enjoyed what little bit she got to see. She stood there in the doorway, peering up at me with those dark eyes that were like deep cave openings, carved out of rock a million years prior, reaching back into time.

She said, "Oh, that's okay. I am used to it. Indian people still get the short end around here sometimes. No one appreciates us. I am Navajo. Do you know the story of the code talkers?"

At that time I didn't. "No, I'm sorry, I don't."

She told me the story of the famous Indian "code talkers" who, during World War II, made a huge contribution to the United States war effort by translating classified allied message traffic into their native tongue and re-sending it where it was re-translated back into English by a Native American on the other end. It utterly confused our enemies because they thought it was indeed some form of code. German and Japanese code breakers alike were totally bewildered, trying to decipher this code that actually was a language they had never heard before and had no reference point from which to translate. Especially in the Pacific, the U.S. would never have been able to pull off some of the successful campaigns it did there without this clever trick.

"I was a code talker," she said abruptly, eyeing me wistfully. "I hope you learn that story someday, young man."

"Well, I hope you get your son back soon," was all I could muster. I turned to walk back to the bus, about to be in the wind headed for California.

"I do, too. Be careful on that bus now . . ." She trailed off, closing the door.

Two days later while coming up the 405 freeway out of San Diego, bound for Sacramento, that bus caught fire in the engine compartment below the rear lounge and burned to the ground right there on the side of the freeway. It burned so fast we had no time to get any belongings out. We stood flattened up against the dividing wall with cars and trucks whooshing by at a frightening pace. The drivers were either honking the horn or making gestures out the window indicating their displeasure at the black smoke from our burning bus polluting their brown smog.

Tree-huggers then, just like now, were strange people. I'm not much of a believer in coincidence, but I think a curse was involved. In her mind, we had trespassed on that elderly woman's sacred land, and were paying the fine for it. I don't think she was crazy at all. The Native American people I have met over the years are all standup folks. Tragically, they are still treated differently, and their history of getting the short end has never been truly told. One story alone—what really happened in 1890 at Wounded Knee, South Dakota—is enough to realize how wronged they were as a people. Despite that story and many other similar examples in the past, I don't know of any Native Americans who overtly capitalize on that history the way race hustlers from other minorities do. Those crackpots do nothing but degrade and disable the very people they supposedly represent. If that proud old gal really was a code talker, then I say to her, "Thanks for your service."

We miraculously made it to Sacramento in a pair of rented station wagons, played the show, and headed north in another leased bus toward the spectacular scenery of the Pacific Northwest.

The show must, and always will, go on.

CHAPTER 18

Livin' On the Edge

One day your life will flash before your eyes. Make sure it's worth watching.

Gerard Way, My Chemical Romance

*   *   *

The band had not been with the label very long when they tasked us with filming a video, announcing us as their new flagship to the music world. The rather bold concept seemed exciting. We were in Las Vegas to open a show at the Aladdin Theatre for the Performing Arts with the Charlie Daniels Band.

The Aladdin Theatre was a little different from the popular casino image. Seating about 7,500, it was done up in the art deco style of early 20th century venues that used to dominate the cities and towns of this country. Absolutely beautiful, it boasted ornate handmade interior elements designed with acoustics in mind, not basketball. These wonderful rooms somehow held time prisoner. Once inside, I could feel the vibe of ghosts and their legendary performances there from long ago.

My grandmother had been a concert pianist with the New York Philharmonic about the time the *Titanic* slipped under the waves of the cold North Atlantic. Believe me when I say I felt her there on stage with me the night we were privileged to play Carnegie. These richly historical places are my favorite venues, both to watch a show and play one. Now, the Aladdin obviously hadn't risen during the Gilded Age, but it was a great replica and it thrilled me to be there.

As a fan, I was excited to be opening for one of my favorites—Charlie Daniels. I was so impressed by how well everybody treated us. Charlie's guys made sure we had everything we needed, sound and equipment-wise. They made sure we felt welcome as a part of the show, something they really didn't have to do. That's Charlie, though, a musician's musician.

We had the next couple of days off, so that's when we started filming our very first video for RCA. From most of the strip in Las Vegas, one can look west and see a formidable ridge of mountains rising off towards the Sierra Nevada range of California. These mountains climb steeply from the desert floor to an elevation above eleven-thousand feet in some places. Snow-capped, even for most of the summer, they form a formidable natural backdrop for all that glitters in Sin City. Standing like sentinels, just before the big mountains to the west, lies a phalanx of gigantic rocks that look like the fingers of a hand held tightly together, jutting up several-thousand feet from the dry, scrub-covered, rolling terrain at their base. About thirty miles outside of town, this was where part of the video would be filmed—not at the base of the cliffs, but *on top* of them.

We had gotten an early start. The band, a couple of road guys, and the video producer loaded into a van and left from the hotel around 8 a.m. I listened as the producer gave us the rundown on the storyline for the video. It would have an old-west theme with us lip-synching parts of "My Home's in Alabama," and "Tennessee River," the two tunes that had put us on the map so far. We would wear distressed western-style clothing and ride horses. A dramatic shot would include a massive confederate flag draped across the cliffs with our band logo and RCA's logo emblazoned on it.

The van ride out to the filming location took about an hour. The lead singer and guitar player were having a little fun at my expense, saying, "Man, I can't wait to see old Herndon on a horse. He's probably never even been in a barn." I didn't say anything. I just smiled to myself and formed a little plan.

I had grown up around horses, but never saw the need to bring it up. They didn't know they were picking on the wrong guy. I learned to ride and show American Saddlebred five-gaited horses by the time I was in fifth grade. My mother was an avid horsewoman who pursued the hobby relentlessly while I was growing up. She taught me to ride and, consequently, I rode many a hot-blooded stallion or mare for her in horse shows. In short, I learned to handle squirrely horses pretty well. I stayed quiet and let the band members keep up their kidding. I had a surprise in store for them.

The western wear/horseback part of the video would be shot first, but the helicopter pilot said the winds were picking up at the top and he couldn't wait until later in the day.

"The pilot of the *what?* What do we need a helicopter for?" I asked.

"It's going to be awesome," the producer said. "You guys up on top of that cliff with the banner splayed out behind you, singing and playing out across the desert like you're singing to the whole world. Get it?"

We had diverted from a dude ranch where the horses were kept, to the helicopter landing zone set up the day before

I got out of the van and stared straight up, three thousand feet, at a sheer rock face stretching upwards into the deep blue of the desert sky. "This is going to be so cool," I said.

I got a couple of blank stares in return.

"Time to saddle up," said the pilot.

I wanted to go first.

He said, "Okay, guys. As I mentioned earlier, the wind is up and it is warmer than forecast, so for the helicopter's sake I can only take two at a time." Not yet rated commercially in helicopters, I didn't question this call.

A band member and I got into the helicopter and strapped in.

The bird was a 1970s model Bell Jet Ranger. The civilian version is underpowered, to say the least. Add some wind with density altitude critical due to the heat and you can be in a tight spot in no time.

We took off, exiting the huge dust cloud we had stirred up, heading north to parallel the rock face, gaining forward speed, then started climbing. The LZ (landing zone) dropped away, along with any concerns I may have had. The city of Vegas lay off to the east in full view, the early morning sun glinting off the glass and steel of the Strip. Lake Mead shimmered farther off to the east, brilliant blue contrasting vividly against the various shades of brown desert stretching off to the horizon.

To my left, the rock face seemed only inches away. The helicopter roared, deafening us because the doors had been taken off for filming. I was in heaven. The ground stretched far below as we banked right to continue the climb, headed south along the wall, halfway up the mocha-colored vertical cliff. The air temperature dropped rapidly. As we crossed over the ridge top, the helicopter lurched in a cold gust of wind fresh off the snowy Sierras not far away. The other band member, not a person who likes to fly, looked white as a ghost.

The pilot continued on the southerly heading for a few moments, then turned back west, now over the top of the small plateau by several hundred feet. He turned east to set up for landing, approaching from the west towards the edge of the cliff, half a mile from touchdown.

I craned my head from the backseat to see, then thought I might be in a bad dream past time to wake up. The LZ was a carport-sized flat space amongst jagged rocks. Four trees, two on each side, framed the little space like sentries.

As we descended, the air started to get really rough. The wind that morning, although calm down below, proved quite strong up here in the place where only an eagle would dwell. Beyond the tiny LZ waited a sheer drop of more than three-thousand feet. The LZ was literally on the edge.

The wind tossed us around like a toy, but the pilot seemed determined. Underpowered, the aircraft didn't have enough muscle to maintain an out-of-ground-effect hover at high altitude, so we couldn't approach the LZ from the east.

Landing with the wind at your back is a no-no in helicopters as well as airplanes, but the guy had no choice except to come in this way. Since he wore a ball cap with a U.S. Army Air Cav patch on it, I figured he had seen a lot worse.

He wrestled the chopper onto the flat rock. It felt more like sliding into home than a landing. He throttled down and, grinning, said he would return with the others.

Some color returned to the other guy's face as we sat there with a couple of video techs, admiring the spectacular view. I crept to the edge and peered over. Down below, the van and a few other vehicles parked around the base LZ looked the size of pinheads.

My head began to swim so, on my hands and knees, I eased back the others.

The other two band members came up on the next run. Watching the helicopter pitch and buck in the disturbed air flow, I began to wonder how long we were going to spend on this plateau in the sky, should the helo go down, God forbid. The pilot followed the same approach path. Right before skids touched rock, a gust pushed him sideways.

I watched in horror as the rotor blade lopped off the top of a pine tree.

Wobbling after the recovery, he miraculously regained control and set her down in the middle of the LZ. I figured he probably had done that many times before, probably with North Vietnamese guys in black pajamas shooting AK-47s at him.

As the engine slowed, one member exited the chopper in great haste and ran away from it. He must have been disoriented from the roller-coaster ride because he started heading in the wrong direction—east—toward that three thousand-foot free fall to the desert below. I don't know if our screaming over the roar of the helicopter got his attention, but he checked up, lost his balance, slipped and fell, then slid towards the abyss. Somehow, he grabbed something that stopped his momentum, maybe two feet from going over. It took a few minutes for everybody to get his color back. Our guy told the pilot to bring him a good strong drink on the next run.

The video crew had flown up the day before to leave the banner at the LZ. Now they worked furiously to unfurl it and get it fastened down in what was becoming a pretty stiff wind.

Chilled to the bone from the wind, freshly cooled by the higher, colder terrain behind us, I gazed around. The snowcapped peaks of the next ridge over looked a lot different from here than from Vegas. Only the tops of trees, all the way to the tree line, poked out of the snow. They looked like big trees, too. Snow in the Rockies is measured in yards deep, not feet or inches.

The chopper appeared again, bouncing in the wind like a dragonfly with a bad gyro. It hung suspended out beyond the edge of the precipice with the cameraman hanging out the door like a gunner. We spent the next hour posing in regal stances, with stern pioneer expressions on our faces, standing in front of the banner for the airborne cameraman dangling out of the helicopter. As the whirlybird made pass after pass just feet from us, trying to get the best shot, the banner dislodged and suddenly took flight.

It disappeared over the side. After a lot of expletives on the walkie-talkies between the cameraman and the grip guys with us, the two in the chopper went looking for it. Unless it went all the way to the ground, I have no clue how they could have retrieved it.

We sat and waited. Finally someone decided to scrap the scene on the cliff. We never found the banner.

The chopper pilot—who I figured was either damn good, crazy, or a little of both—flew down to the desert LZ and dropped off the cameraman. He came back to start extracting us, two by two, from the top. He landed, fighting the turbulence much the same as before. I was on the first lift out. He brought the throttle up and, with engine screaming, pushed the stick forward, pulled pitch, and skidded that bird right off the rock and out into space. Strapped tightly in my seat, the sight of ground falling from a mere couple of feet to thousands in an instant, is something I will never forget. He flung that copter out into thin air and, for a moment, I thought I had left my stomach behind.

I wondered if the ensuing crash would make the news and how it would sound.

We dropped a good hundred feet due to the curling effect of wind flowing across the edge. Somehow, underneath the downdraft, the rotor caught lift and we clawed away from the giant wall behind us. Now in undisturbed air, we enjoyed a smooth ride all the way down to the lower and much safer LZ.

Two more just-as-harrowing trips later, he landed with both guys from the video company amongst some very relieved musicians and support personnel. With no time to worry, we just had to shake it off. The show, as always, must go on. We had to beat feet to the scene location to stay on schedule. I started to smile.

That next scene was on horseback.

We moved to the dude ranch a couple of miles away. The label had negotiated to film in the rustic, weather-beaten collection of stables, cabins, and restaurant-plus-bar for patrons wanting a rugged-west outdoor experience, complete with guided horseback tours out in the desert. When we got there and stepped out of the van, the producer said we had a few minutes to relax while they prepared the next set.

I noticed some very attractive female extras on set, so I started chatting with one or two. I felt quite macho, relating my recent tale of near death high in the Rockies. The girls "oohed" and "ahhed" at all the right places.

I pondered inviting them back to the hotel, but the producer pulled me aside and whispered, "Just saying . . . be careful man. Those ladies are professional, if you know what I mean."

Oh, yeah, that's right. I remembered we were in Nevada, after all. "Got it." I wandered off in search of the horse wrangler, my little plan for some fun back in focus.

"Gimme the hottest horse you got," I said to the wrangler on the other side of the barn from the others. He had already saddled up four old-and-slow trail horses for our horseback scene.

"All we got are these old plugs," he said.

Covering my background riding show horses, I explained what I wanted to do. "What about yours?" I asked.

Now, asking a cowboy to give up his horse is akin to asking a soldier to surrender his weapon, but I was naïve about a lot of things back then, so I pressed on. Reluctantly agreeing, he dismounted.

I mounted up, we adjusted the stirrups, and I guess I convinced him it wasn't my first time on a horse. He started grinning and went along with it.

I waited till the other three were helped onto their respective plugs. I had delayed just long enough for the producer to wonder if I had run off with one of the working girls, just long enough for the guys to get irritated that I had gone missing.

I collected the reins, clucked to the wrangler's horse, and moved into view. As I got closer, I signaled the horse with one rein and pushed my toe into his right side to get him to sidestep towards the shocked group. This was a good horse. He pranced as if showing in a parade. I switched reins and toes, and he sidestepped the other way, his big nostrils flaring and snorting for great effect. I rode him to about ten yards from the little group watching in total silence. I stopped him and applied a little backpressure on both reins while digging my heels into his sides. That got him to do the *Hi-yo, Silver* thing. He pawed the air, and I released the reins as he dropped back to all fours.

Astride his horse, Jeff just burst out laughing, followed by some of the others. Randy didn't say a word. He just shook his head, maybe having his first second-thoughts about me being in the band. I had tears in my eyes from having to hold back laughing myself. I returned the cutting horse to the wrangler and, feeling ten feet tall, mounted my trail horse for the next segment.

We filmed several different angles for what seemed like forever. We would ride a few yards for the camera, stop and get off. They would move the horses back and we would do it all over again. This went on and on.

Finally, we took a break. We moved to the bar for the band performance onstage, while the rest of the crew set up for the final shot outside—us, back on the horses again, clad in our hats and dusters riding off into the sunset, of course.

Positioned in front of a little rise close to the buildings, we mounted up in a line like the Four Horsemen of the Apocalypse. We were supposed to ride look-ing intense, as we solemnly rode off into parts unknown, off to new horizons, off to save the . . . whatever.

It sounded cheesy, but it always worked in those old western movies, right?

Just as the director called "Action!" that damn helicopter rose up from be-hind the little hill and flew right at us. I guess the "off into the sunset" shot needed an aerial angle, too.

The wranglers grabbed two of the musicians' horses.

Mine spooked a little, but I dismounted and held his head with the reins.

One musician's horse took off with him on it, bolting from the helicopter at a gallop. He was bouncing around to the side of the saddle, holding on for dear life, yelling, "Whoa! Whoa! Shit! I said, 'Whoa' damn it!" For all we could tell, he had single-handedly resurrected the Pony Express. That horse carried him half a mile before the horseback wranglers caught up. When they stopped his horse, he fell the rest of the way off, a little cloud of dust puffing up around him to mark the spot.

I don't know what happened to that video. The whole thing turned out to be a waste of time, really. The label never used what we were able to film. Things happen on the learning curve, and it was a steep one for all of us in those days. The band learned the value of maintaining control over image marketing—and safety, for that matter.

Always have a hand in the concept and design of videos.

CHAPTER 19

The Music Mill

I played on very few of the band's records: "Travelin' Shoes," "I'm Not That Way Anymore" and "Christmas in Dixie" are a few where I did. I remember one, though, in particular.

The band had really taken off about this time. Pressure from the label to come up with hits came thick and heavy. The vibe around the studio felt pretty intense most of the time we were tracking. Time is money. I didn't have much studio experience when I came on board. I had always learned new songs the way most musicians do, by going over the material many times in rehearsal. Studio time is not cheap, which means very little rehearsal. We toured three-hundred days a year, so nobody wanted to woodshed when we got home.

Harold Shedd, the producer then, would line up a group of Nashville session players who could listen to a demo, chart it, go in the studio, and usually nail it down in just a few takes—cost effective, to say the least. They could usually do three or four songs a day this way. This still amazes me. It takes many rehearsals and many times playing a new song in front of a crowd to get it truly right, doing it the traditional way.

One night during a break, we all sat around the studio, just hanging out. Some sort of scheduling problem with the next session meant the players would be late. The lead singer pulled out a song he had been working on and started playing it on his acoustic guitar for Harold.

We'd had pizza and beers delivered, so everyone felt relaxed and in a good mood. The tune proved catchy, so I joined in to play along with a pair of sticks on the back of the couch. It all came naturally. We had fun.

Perhaps it was the beers, or the vibe, or whatever; but Harold recognized the freshness of the moment. He said, "Let's run a take right now."

That surprised me. All four of us went into the studio and plugged in. In the drum booth, I sat at the kit used for the previous session.

Through the headphones, I heard Harold say, "All right, guys. Just do it like you were doing it before."

I counted it off and everything seemed to flow like magic right from the start. I didn't have to think about an arrangement, the parts seemed to define themselves in my head before I came to them. Nobody had to direct or suggest anything. It just happened.

I think all four of us were on the same wavelength that night. When we finished playing what I felt would be a good demo for the session guys to "improve" on later, Harold's voice came over the headphones. "Wow. I think y'all ought to come in here and listen. Don't think we gonna get any better than that."

That little jam turned out to be "Mountain Music," one of the group's greatest hits.   What you hear on that record was done in one take. It captured what made that band the top concert draw for so many years—energy.

That studio was The Music Mill, owned by our producer, Harold Shedd. It still stands today, an abandoned and forgotten brick building at the edge of a parking lot near Music Row.

Harold would go on to build a bigger state-of-the-art studio in Nashville by the same name. The band continued to record with him for several more albums there. His talent for visualizing a song and communicating those ideas in simple language made for a truly great producer. Harold always offered a calming presence in the middle of a high-pressure situation. Sometimes, even under the pressure of deadlines, the funniest things could happen . . .

I remember one afternoon at The Music Mill, I was sitting with the sound engineer behind the console in one of the control rooms. The other three band members, along with several studio pickers, were hashing out an arrangement in the studio. A tall stately woman by the name of Francis Preston walked in. She had heard we were in town tracking, so she came by to say "hi" to us. Back then, Francis was the president of BMI, the largest music-publishing firm in the world. She was also our friend.

Needless to say, I felt honored that such a VIP would want to come by and look in on us.

Francis defined graciousness. She oozed class and worldliness. She also had tremendous clout, not only in Nashville, but also in other music towns such as New York, Los Angeles, and London. Sophisticated and powerful, she never acted arrogant.

She brought a half-dozen or so staffers from BMI with her, two or three of them female. Unbeknownst to her, the session had not been going to well for the troupe. With tempers on edge, it was a good time to take a break. All but one of the core members came out of the session to say hello. I guess nobody told him about her. He and the engineer focused on getting a certain tone out of his instrument. They kept trying and trying, but to no avail. He was getting really frustrated. He had about had it.

The engineer pressed the talkback and made a suggestion. "You need more bottom end in that sound; try something else."

From where he sat in the studio, he couldn't see the gathering in the control room. As far as he knew, it was just us, the engineer, and Harold. Sometimes even at your wits end, a little humor comes into play. He turned around, stuck his ass up to the mic, and said, "How's this for bottom end?"

What exploded from the speakers in the crowded control room is the stuff of legends. Flatulence that would have made a grain-fed mule jealous pealed from the woofers like thunder. Not just a quick staccato burst, this. Oh no. This massive fart summed up the whole day so far. A long, moaning, low-note, sixteen-bar solo of epic tone, exasperation and intensity hurled through the monitors for all present to witness.

As they say . . . a hush fell over the room. The clock stopped ticking. I don't remember how long the silence lasted. It seemed like eternity. It seemed funny as hell, but out of respect to the iconic Francis Preston, nobody dared laugh. Everyone in the room stood paralyzed.

Finally, one of the other members got on the interphone and said calmly, "Uh . . . hey . . . Francis Preston is here to see us, so why don't you come in here and say 'hi.'?"

The bandmate who made so much noise looked around the corner, froze, and dropped like a rock behind one of the sound baffles. I thought he'd had a heart attack.

Well, Francis, in true world-class fashion, stood there motionless for a minute. She let the room sizzle for just the perfect amount of time. She walked over to the mixing console, expressionless, pressed the talk-back button, and with perfect delivery said, "Bottom end is important. I think you're on to something there."

The room erupted. Everyone was doubled over. We all laughed until the tears ran. After a few minutes, someone noticed that he still hadn't come in to say hi to Francis and her entourage. I went into the studio and looked around the baffle where I had seen him vanish, but he was gone. He must have belly-crawled out the back door and run off like a rabbit, because nobody saw him for the rest of the day.

We had quite a few laughs later, but it really bothered the old boy for a while. It would have me, too, but damn, it was funny. I wish we could have put a little something for Francis in the liner notes on that album.

I know she would have laughed, too.

CHAPTER 20

Girls, Girls, Girls

In the '80s, if you were in a band, especially a well-known band, even if you had skinny arms and legs and looked weird like I did at the time, you would have had no problem with the ladies. If you were single like I was, you could get hooked up just about any night. The women would literally throw themselves at you.

Now, I never professed to be a saint, so I enjoyed this attention. I was very wary of many of them, though. A paternity-suit scenario always lurked in the back of my mind. Over the years I heard such stories, and to tell the truth I hadn't forgotten entirely about my night of adventure with Beth back in college days. Sure, I was a red-blooded young buck and had a good time with some, but for some reason, the times I remember most are the times when I expected to get lucky, but old Murphy's Law would interfere.

We were in Daytona playing at the Speedway as part of a huge music festival. More than a hundred thousand filled the stands. The promoters provided helicopters to ferry the performers back and forth from the show to the hotels where everybody stayed. Really big time, it was exciting. We were the headliner, thus scheduled to go on last that night around 10:00.

After I stepped off the helicopter, crew showed me to the backstage area. Twenty-five or thirty buses lined up behind the stage, countless tractor-trailer rigs farther back, their engines on high idle, creating a rumbling, rhythmic *thrum, thrum, thrum.* The low frequency drone served as a subliminal sonic backdrop to the electricity in the air. Finding my way through the myriad generator trucks with miles of cables snaking in every direction, I made it back to catering and the dressing room area.

After only a few minutes, I found myself in pleasant conversation with a gorgeous girl working as a production assistant to one of the TV crews. She called herself Andrea. We had about an hour before the show to sit and chat. I found myself attracted to her. Very sexy, she showed a lot of mischief in her eyes.

Still the 1980s, we were young. She said she had finished work for the night, but wanted to stay and see our show. She was obviously attracted to me, too.

"Of course," I said, "I will get you a stage pass to hang out stage left and get a great view." Stage left had the best view of the drum riser, naturally. "If you don't have plans, why don't you stay after we get done and I'll find us a party or something."

"Sounds great!" she gushed, winking her eye seductively.

Uh-oh.

The show over, I quickly determined she was still hanging out, so I hurried back from the dressing room after drying off and changing clothes. I had the big head strutting her around to a couple of after-show parties in full swing aboard a few of the buses behind the stage.

When we had enough drinks to embolden our new friendship, she wanted to go to my hotel "for a nightcap."

Phew!

Like I said, a beautiful lady, me twenty-something and young and free and well . . . what's a fella to do? Suddenly I remembered the helicopter. Now I could look like a real big shot.

We lifted off in a swirl of noise and blowing dust, climbing away from the Daytona Speedway bathed in lights. The grandstands were emptying rapidly now that the event had ended. Long snakes of red taillights stretching every direction from the track showed the traffic jam our privilege let us avoid.

Andrea and I sat in the back, taking in the lights of high-rise hotels lining the beach. The beach! An idea formed in my rather buzzed mind. I leaned forward and asked the pilot if he could land us there.

"Not a problem, bud," he hollered over the piercing whine of the jet engine spinning the rotor just above our heads. We flew over the hotels and out over the water for a little way while he picked out a spot. Daytona Beach is really wide, so he didn't have to look for long. He set us down on the south side of the pier, about three-hundred yards from my hotel, away from its lights shining on the beach. The pilot and I must have been thinking the same thing.

We stood watching as he took off again, whirring away into the night, leaving us in sudden welcomed silence after so much noise and hustle-bustle. The air felt warm and balmy as the surf gently broke around the pier. Nobody ventured out at this hour; we found ourselves alone.

The combination of romantic setting and the fires of youthful desire made various pieces of clothing fall from our bodies. Giggling and naked, we ran into the water. Things got pretty frisky; soon thereafter, Andrea decided we should finish what we started in the privacy of a room. I didn't object at this point, paternity suits be damned . . . I led her back to the beach to get our clothes. We stepped out of the frothy surf and . . .

"Oh my god," Andrea said. "Our clothes are gone."

I looked around. She was right. I don't know how long we had been in the water, but it must have been long enough for the tide or a wave with gusto to pull our garments down to Davey Jones's Locker.

I headed down the beach in my birthday suit. Just enough ambient light from the stars and hotel lights behind us helped me spy what looked like some material bunched up and floating in the shallows. I grabbed it and shook it out.

"That's my dress," Andrea said.

I handed it to her and she wrapped up.

I wasn't so lucky. We never found anything of mine.

Feeling rather sheepish and not so stud-like, I started to wonder how the hell I was going to get back to my room. "Let's go up under the pier and I'll figure something out," I said. This was in the days before cell phones, so I had no way to "phone a friend."

As we walked up to where the pier joined the embankment, I spotted a large cardboard box shoved up under the decking on the pier. It had been there a long time, wet and now rather fragile. I pulled it down and, after unfolding it, fashioned a wrap-around. It just barely covered my mid-section. I breathed a small sigh of relief. Lots better than in the buff.

Andrea clutching her torn, saltwater-soaked dress together with one hand and me wearing the box, we headed toward the hotel. We met a few people on the beach who seemed just as buzzed as we were. They laughed and jeered at us as we stumbled up the stairs. We had to go through the lobby because all the side doors were locked and now, without pants or wallet, I had to somehow get a key.

Talk about making an entrance! When we walked into the lobby sporting our fashion statement, it was still full of fans lingering around, hoping to catch a glimpse of one of the band members.

Well, they did.

I was recognized right off the bat. I thought it actually hilarious. If Facebook had been around then, I think the photos would have gone viral. I felt a little embarrassed, but not much. After all, this is the life of a rock star, right? Andrea was laughing too, so I made my way over to the front desk. It got even funnier.

The clerk would not give me a key because I didn't have any identification on me. The supervisor came out front and, after several fans came to my rescue by verifying my identity, I finally got my key. What a sight. We stood there, Andrea's dress dripping a pool of water on the floor and me signing a few autographs, making sure I had a good grip on the ends of my box. After laughing some more with those fans, we trundled off to the elevator and, at last, disappeared from view as the doors whooshed shut.

On the way up, our amorous desires returned. I led her to my room, fumbled with the key, and unlocked the door. I still had one more hurdle to jump. I did not have a room to myself. The hotel had put our pilot, Larry, in with me due to shortage of rooms. No biggie. We often roomed together for flight-operations convenience in those days. However, tonight proved a bit awkward. At least we had a two-bedroom suite.

I opened the door to a pitch-black room. Larry slept soundly in the other room, his door ajar.

Andrea dropped her dress on the floor and lay on the bed. I joined her, full of anticipation. Just as we stopped giggling about our grand entrance to the hotel, a tremendous fart echoed from the other room, followed by a cough and Larry rolling over in his sleep.

"What was that?" Andrea squawked as she sprang off the bed, grabbing her dress.

"Ugh, well, uhmm, it's our pilot, Larry," I said, wincing.

"Who the hell—what kind of girl do you think I am?"

Thinking about how she had flown in a helicopter with a guy she just met, then swam with him butt-naked in shark-infested waters, followed by a scantily clad parade through the hotel lobby, I said, "A pretty damn cool one."

It didn't impress her. "You must be some kind of pervert or something!"

"I was planning on shutting his door" I said, but shouldn't have.

"Well, I'm not doing anything with that man in there. Gawd!" She ran into the bathroom to blow her dress with the hairdryer.

She came out after a while, wearing the dress.

Now, I'm not a perv, and I knew the night had come to an abrupt stop as far as getting to know her any better.

I slung on a pair of sweats and said, "I will get you a cab home. I'm really sorry." The song "What's Your Name?" by Skynyrd flashed through my brain, and I almost laughed out loud. I woke Larry and borrowed some cash. I gave it to her for the cab.

As she opened the door to go, she said, "Look, I didn't mean to be a bitch. I really like you. I just got really embarrassed for some reason. Maybe we can get together next time you're in town."

Thinking with a clearer head now, I didn't see where the embarrassment thing added up. She'd been eager to swim naked in public earlier. Oh well, we both had had too much to drink.

I said, "Sounds good; stop by and give me a shout then," or something goofy like that.

About a year later, Andrea showed up at the hotel where we stayed for the stop in Daytona again. I ran into her in the lobby, of all places.

She gave me a little hug and said, "Come outside; there's somebody I want you to meet."

Figuring a jealous boyfriend, I walked over to her car with a little trepidation. Another girl sat in the front, and a baby seat in the back had an infant buckled in.

"This is Jason," she said.

I said hi to the other girl. "Cute kid. Congrats, Mom."

"Oh, he's not mine," she said. "He's Andrea's."

I did the math and, remembering the night a year ago, almost passed out.

Andrea laughed and said, "Good thing your buddy was in the room, huh?"

She must have found someone else who liked late-night swims in the ocean, I reckon. I learned that old Murphy can sometimes be a friend in disguise, even when you might be cussing him at the time.

"Phew!" is all I can say.

CHAPTER 21

The Warrior Class

Among the many codes of the road in the entertainment business, one I have mentioned before drives performers to take unimaginable risks, sometimes just to get to the next show. Among the codes we live by is one that, although never really said out loud, is exemplified in performance and deeds, done above and beyond mere obligation, by talent and support people alike. Under great duress at times, much like members of the military who live by the unspoken code of "mission first," we get the job done no matter what. It bonds us deeply, sometimes, even if to outsiders we don't always seem to get along.

In the mid-1980s a segment of the tour took us to twenty or so military installations throughout the Southwest. Soon the last leg of these shows would end in California. I really enjoyed these concerts. The service people we entertained from Texas to the West Coast showed their appreciation like nothing I had ever experienced. Whenever and wherever we would perform for them, not only would the crowds be wonderful, but the folks tasked with hospitality and event coordination would take us in like one of their own. Thrilled that we showed interest in and appreciation for what they were doing, they always went many, many extra miles for us in such selfless ways.

We played an afternoon show at the Navy base in San Diego. The opening act had finished their set, and our crew was busy getting the stage ready for us. The base commander, a Navy SEAL, had come back to the dressing room to say hello before we went on. Excitement and anticipation from the crowd out front filled the air. Energy spilled over the stage and back into the dressing room as we shared some laughs and stories with him. Built like a fireplug without an ounce of flab anywhere, he and his animated command presence electrified the room.

It came time to head for the stage. Grinning, he shook everyone's hands, thanked us again and again for coming, and gave everybody an enthusiastic pat on the back as we headed out the door. I imagined he had done this many times before, patting the backs of his fellow SEALS going out the breach of a C-130 aircraft as they jumped into an unknown fate from thirty-thousand feet, parachuting into the void.

Outside now and fired up, I headed past a security checkpoint manned by an MP holding a very intimidating German Shepard police dog. Tight security was

SOP on military bases everywhere we played. I eyed it warily, a fleeting thought of running from MPs like this long ago crossing my mind. The handler had the animal on a tight leash, so I quickly forgot my worry, listening to the roar of ten-thousand sailors and Marines there for a party.

I bounded up the stairs, really ready to rock. As I got to the top, the stage manager held up his hand, telling me to stop. "Hold up, Mark" he said. His walkie-talkie was blaring something, but I couldn't hear what due to the crowd noise. I was the only band member up on stage.

"What's the problem?" I asked.

"Stand down, stand down! Hold the intro track! Roll more walk in!" he yelled into his radio.

Damn. Just when things were about get really fun, we have some freaking technical problem and it's a buzz kill for the crowd, I thought to myself.

I looked toward the bottom of the stairs as somebody motioned me to come down. I didn't need encouragement. I felt kind of stupid, standing there by myself with no one else to make noise with. I started toward the dressing room. There, behind the stage Teddy sat in a heap on the ground with a crowd of medics and base personnel surrounding him. I ran up and saw him ashen faced and bleeding rather profusely from the right arm.

My heart sank.

What the hell happened? Thinking he had fallen, somehow, I asked one of the medics.

"Dog got away from the handler. If your bass player hadn't had his hand in the air, waving to those people, he would have got it in the throat."

JEEEZUS! What? This could be really bad. There's no way a guy can play bass with his right arm mauled, I thought.

The medics helped Teddy up, then escorted him to the dressing room. We all followed in, fearing the worst.

Now in shock, with his arm still bleeding pretty badly, he let them lay him on a cot. He was white as a ghost, but calm, considering what had just happened.

Worried, I stepped outside to listen to what would be announced to the rowdy crowd. After a brief announcement of delay followed by a few boos, I went back inside. Teddy was now sitting upright with a shot of whiskey in his hand, even joking a little with the medics.

The base commander burst into the dressing room, wanting to know the extent of the wounds. I thought the guy would implode; he was so mad and embarrassed at the same time.

The dog's teeth had penetrated both sides of the forearm about halfway down from the elbow and met in the middle—four deep puncture wounds, plus some shredding of muscle tissue from yanking on the arm before the handler regained control. It wasn't a pretty sight.

After a pull on his drink, Teddy shook off the effects of shock, wiggled his fingers on the injured arm, and said, "Hell, wrap it up boys. I'll play."

One of the medics recommended the opposite. "You can do permanent harm to your arm because we don't know if there is nerve damage or not."

"I said wrap it up, damn it. I'm good." He grimaced.

As we walked out to start the show again—no dogs of any kind within a hundred miles—another announcement described exactly what happened and said we would play anyway. This brought the house down. The warriors in that crowd loved it. I reckon they could identify with it, in a way: wounded, but still in the fight.

Man, I was very proud of Teddy as he held up his bandaged arm to thunderous cheers from the Navy crowd and OOrahs! from the Marines. To them that day, at least one celebrity wasn't a pussy. We rocked their socks off. We had become one with them and they with us, because we both lived by codes that are rather similar.

That night, during a small after-show ceremony in the Officers Club, the base commander, who twenty years earlier had been gravely wounded in Southeast Asia as a patrol-boat gunner, eloquently presented Teddy his own Purple Heart. He had been awarded the medal during action in the sweltering Mekong Delta region of South Vietnam.

Teddy respectfully declined, but the SEAL officer would have none of it. He actually pinned it on him, more cheers and OOrahs! coming from the room.

The arm healed on its own. They shot him full of antibiotics, and we went on about the business of endless touring soon after.

Ever humble and knowing the medal rightfully belonged to the heroic base commander, Teddy mailed it back to him about a month later with a letter, saying in good conscience he could not keep it. I imagine upon receiving it, this fine officer immediately started the process of sending it back with orders to keep it. We will never know. Tragically, this decorated hero died not long afterwards in a car crash off base. What a loss.

Teddy made us all look good that day to people we respected to the utmost. We felt the privilege of a brief camaraderie with the warrior class, and I got a glimpse of what true class really is.

I felt so much richer for it.

CHAPTER 22

Unsung Heroes

Speaking of the warrior class, I would be beyond remiss if I didn't mention the guys who made up our road crew. We never would have been able to do the myriad things we did if not for them. From the day we left the Bowery, taking some bartenders and waiters we'd come to know with us as crew, to working with a full-time staff of forty-plus on the last show of the American Farewell Tour ending in 2004, we had the finest in the business. In my opinion, the legacy of the band, still talked about in venues across the country to this day, is the heroic things the guys and girls did to make sure the show was always up and ready to go on time. Against all odds, sometimes, they never failed to make us look good.

We never missed a show because of technical or logistic problems for more than 25 years. Countless stories of working like dogs as much as eighteen to twenty hours a day, three or four hours' rest, then doing it all again could fill the pages of another book. They missed time with their families more than we did in the heyday, many times because we had the band's airplane to go home on breaks while the crew kept chugging on to make the next series of dates. A few got hurt. A few got sick. A few even had nervous breakdowns from the stress and relentless pace we all had to keep up. No one ever complained. Everybody pulled his weight. I loved many of these guys, and I am still lifelong friends with some. Of all the heroic stories of their unique dedication, one at this moment comes to mind.

We stopped in Oshkosh, Wisconsin, for a huge, multi-act outdoor festival in the late '90s. I rose from my rack that morning with an intangible-but-creepy feeling in my gut. Several years later, I would have the same feeling getting in my bunk while traveling across the Arizona desert towards Las Vegas in the wee hours of Sept 11, 2001. I have learned to respect these strange premonitions.

We had the best drivers, too—millions of miles and not a single wreck amongst them. Sure, we had a few close calls and some minor scrapes on paint, but nothing major—ever. At one time we had ten tractor-trailers and seven buses out for more than 180 days a year, steady. Go figure the odds of an accident there.

After the airplane was sold in '93 to cut rising costs, I returned to riding the crew bus as I had been doing before we started flying. How and why I wound up there in the first place is a story in itself, and I will get to that in a later chapter. I promise.

Del Rucks drove the crew bus. From Rainsville, Alabama, veteran long-haul truck driver Del boasted more than forty years' experience. It seemed like he knew every freeway, secondary highway, and pig trail in North America by heart. He had the touch it takes to haul very fatigued people hundreds of miles every night, giving us sound sleep without worry, pushing onward through the dark of night in all kinds of weather. As a person, he is one of the finest men I have known. "Papa," as we called him affectionately, took care of the bus and his crew like a good skipper looks after his ship and men. We loved him for the example of decency he set, and the many extra things he did, looking out for his employer and us. They truly don't make them like that very often. I am proud to have known him.

I stepped off the bus onto the turf of the Oshkosh Fairgrounds, deserted at this early morning hour, except for the activity around the massive stage nearby. Road cases were rattling down ramps, making that all too familiar tell-tale *zzzzzzzeh, zzzzzzzeh* sound of casters rolling over the tiny traction ridges on loading ramps extended out the back doors of trailers lined up next to the stage.

Blinking the sleep from my eyes, I headed over to catering, the wafting tendrils of fresh coffee smell pulling me in. I usually loved mornings like this, the energy of why we were here already starting to circulate, enhanced by the rhythm of the well-practiced load-in routine. I couldn't shake the monkey, though. I drank a couple of cups, grabbed a biscuit, and headed back to the bus about a hundred yards away. The overcast high above was smooth and ash grey, with the sun barely penetrating it, looking like a cold silver orb. The conditions made my foreboding even worse.

Ugh! Maybe a bike ride will shake it off, I thought.

As I rounded the bus parked in front of ours to get my 12-speed out of the cargo bay, a paramedic shut the rear doors on an ambulance parked at the door. He hurriedly got in the vehicle, turned on the flashing lights, and drove off quickly across the grounds, headed for the gate.

"What's the matter? Somebody got the pukinshits?" I asked the first guy I saw. Food poisoning is an ever-present threat to everyone who lives on the road.

Concern and shock knotting his face up, our production manager, Brent, said, "No, man. Papa's had a stroke."

It felt like a gut punch. "Oh my God, no!" I said.

"Yeah, he got up and just fell over. He was the only one on here. I came back from the stage and found him struggling to breathe on the floor. No telling how long he'd been there."

I went inside the bus and sat. I was numb. Someone I had grown very close to might possibly not be here anymore. Brent followed me.

"Is he still breathing?" I asked. "Yeah, but barely. I got to go make some calls," he said as he left, headed back across the grounds to the backstage office.

A million things run through your mind during times like this, especially reminding you that you are very far from home. We would find out more on Del later.

With his departure, events would now begin to unfurl, leading to one of the most heroic and largely untold lifesaving stories on the road that I have ever heard. My life was going to be one of the many saved.

My dire feeling of dread was not without reason that day. Del was taken to the hospital and stabilized, then flown home for treatment and therapy in Birmingham.

It overjoyed us when the report came later that day saying he would make it. But the curse, demon, bad juju, or whatever it was that draped itself over the show site that day would linger on.

Right before showtime, a tremendous thunderstorm bore down on the field. One-hundred mile-per-hour straight-line winds picked up everything that wasn't nailed down and sent it flying. Missiles of all sizes and shapes knifed through the air, injuring spectators and damaging equipment. The rain came in sheets, raking across the fans running for cover. Two or more inches of water stood everywhere within minutes. I watched the storm lash the fairgrounds from the questionable safety of the bus, rocking like a ship at sea.

The crew guys desperately held on to critical pieces of gear we depended on to make our living. The lighting truss over the stage came down in a huge crash of groaning metal and flying sparks.

I knew we surely had somebody hurt, so I made a run for the stage. I don't know what I could have done, but damn!—those were my friends out there!

About the time I reached the stage area, soaking wet, the mighty elements abated. The wind ceased almost as suddenly as it had come up, and the rain slacked off to a drizzle.

Around what was left of the stage-left P.A. stack, I walked towards the stairs that led up to stage level. The remnants of twisted, broken lighting truss lay helter-skelter, all blinking and hissing behind the stage, dying.

Miraculously, nobody got hurt, but everybody was shaken up. These guys had been through many outdoor shows that turned into rain events, but no one had ever seen a storm so ferocious come up so quickly. The best thing for me to do was stay out of the way and let them do their jobs, so I headed back to the bus. Sitting in the front lounge, watching a movie to kill time, I wondered how we would make it to the next show. I started thinking, at least there can't be anything else bad happen today.

I was wrong.

Just then, another ambulance with lights ablaze and siren wailing zipped by the bus windshield, going toward where the stage stood, now missing its towering lights and roof.

Oh God, they've found someone under the truss, I thought. I took off back to where I was about an hour earlier.

This time the news was grim.

As crew loaded various soaking-wet sections of the stage into one of the trucks, an accident had happened. The floor of the trailers were soaked, the stage soaked, the soles of everybody's shoes soaked—a slippery dangerous mess.

As always, pressure to get to the next town subconsciously, dangerously, hurried people on with their tasks. Promoters often use local people who volunteer to help as stagehands during big events like this one. While helping steady a one-ton set-cart stacked with decking, a young female stagehand slipped on the slick trailer floor and fell.

The set-cart, having a high center of gravity, started to topple over onto her.

Already in the truck, her teenage boyfriend, also a volunteer, saw what was about to happen and shoved her out of the way. He lost his balance and fell as the whole ton of decking came down on him, crushing him.

He died on the spot.

I will never forget my feeling upon seeing this tragedy. *Maybe it's time to quit this shit. Maybe it's time we hang it up. Maybe somebody is trying to tell us something.*

The power-outage darkness surrounding the fairgrounds suddenly seemed to be made of cast iron, pressing in all around the scene, weighing heavy on every square inch of everything. In one day our beloved bus captain ended up in a hospital bed, fighting to live; a storm wrecked hundreds of thousands of dollars' worth of high-tech equipment and injured dozens of concert-goers . . .

And an eighteen-year-old boy lost his life heroically, but needlessly.

Everything can change in a New York minute.

I didn't sleep well that night. None of us would for the next three months because of what started the next day.

We made it to the next town, Milwaukee, by using a crewmember who happened to have a CDL.

CHAPTER 23

Life Savers

After the show in Milwaukee, we picked up a relief driver, the polar opposite of Del. He was flown in by the bus company. His arrival could have spelled doom for us all if it hadn't been for an act done by a couple of our guys who, like many of them over the years, in my opinion, earned a spot within the warrior class. This time, high in the mountains of Northern California, it was nothing less than a miracle from God.

Two months had passed since the unfortunate day at Oshkosh. The atmosphere had never really improved on our bus since Del's departure, largely in part to the incompetence of the relief driver. The guy didn't give us much rest, swerving and driving erratically all the time. He never took care of the bus or looked after us like the many ways Del did. Maybe Del spoiled us somewhat, but people don't realize just how important a good bus driver can be on a tour. Everything, including morale, goes south without adequate rest.

The relief driver, whom I will call "Mac," was getting worse the longer he stayed out with us. Many times at night, driving to the next port, he would seem impaired while driving. We couldn't put a finger on what was wrong. Nobody ever smelled alcohol or anything else on him, but something wasn't right. He seemed groggy all the time. Odd, considering he was supposed to be rested up from sleeping at the hotel room during the day.

We had to take turns staying up, riding the jump seat up front, in order to make sure he didn't fall asleep at the wheel. One person would give up precious rest pulling two hours of guard duty in the jump seat, then go back and wake the next guy for his two-hour shift. We did not have fun, to say the least. Our production manager requested another replacement time and time again, but he got one bullshit excuse after another from the bus company, as well as the band's business manager back in Fort Payne. Mac's daily rate was slightly cheaper than the standard rate.

First clue.

One night, headed south through the high country of Northern California, somewhere around Mt. Shasta, the results of procrastination, pinching pennies, negligence, or a combination thereof, would finally change all this foolishness. I was asleep in my bunk thanks to a new prescription on the market called Ambien.

I had to take it to get some semblance of rest during the rolling, jerking, thrill ride provided by Mac's horrible driving. The next morning, I crawled out of my rack and headed to catering, meeting some very somber faces. The other bus and truck drivers sipped coffee, shaking their heads and talking in hushed voices. I knew something really serious was happening—or had happened. The drivers related to me a story I couldn't believe.

Apparently Mac had become unresponsive on the CB channel the bus drivers used to communicate with each other during the long hauls at night. After trying unsuccessfully to reach him on the radio, the other crew bus driver behind us accelerated to run parallel beside of our bus. We were on a long descending straight stretch of road,-a four lane with wide paved shoulders on the right side and a concrete divider on the left. That kind of road is where you see RUNAWAY TRUCK RAMP—One Mile or STEEP GRADE 8% TRUCKS USE LOWER GEAR signs posted regularly.

The other crew bus driver, Joey, peered into the front section of our bus He could see Mac just staring straight ahead, in a trance.

Mac finally looked over at Joey, slack jawed.

Joey signaled him to pick up his radio mic, but he just turned away, unresponsive.

Mac's dome light was on over his head, so Joey could see him nodding and slumping over the wheel, only to snatch himself awake. Only a few miles remained before the straight road would turn into a winding one. We were hurtling down the mountain at eighty miles an hour.

Beyond the edge of the pavement stood a flimsy guardrail that would not be able to keep a thirty-ton bus from plunging over the steep ravine and falling a thousand feet into a river rushing over giant rock formations below. Terrified now, Joey radioed the situation to one of the truck drivers, David "Griff" Griffin, behind us.

With one last look at Mac, now drooling from his open mouth under the dome light, Joey moved ahead into position in front of our bus.

Griff eased his big, eighty-ton rig right up to the back of our bus at the same time.

Joey slowed gradually, until the nose of our bus made contact with the back of his.

At that moment, coordinating with Joey by radio, the truck driver eased the front of his truck against the rear of our speeding twelve-man coffin.

Together they started slowing down, forcing our bus to do the same, sandwiched between them. It took more than a mile to finally reduce the speed enough to where they could start guiding our bus over to the side.

About this time, Mac came out of whatever hypnotic state he was in—startled out of his wits, I imagine. He applied the brakes and together all three vehicles came to a rather bumpy stop on the shoulder.

Now around 4:00 in the morning, we had barely missed becoming an early-morning news flash.

The place where we stopped was only a half-mile from where the road began to curve. At eighty miles per hour, it would have been about twenty seconds before we would have left the pavement. I had slept through it all due to the sleep aid. For some reason, probably fatigue, we didn't have anyone up with Mac that night, either. Some of the others awoke about the time Mac did, due to the rough stop—a stop that was much better than the one we would've had at the bottom of the rocky gorge.

The other drivers said Mac was babbling and delirious when they came to see what was wrong. He was relieved of duty by Joey, the other drivers, and a few of the crew guys, promptly on the spot. I don't think extraction from the driver's seat was a pleasant experience for Mac.

At least, I hope it wasn't.

An extra driver from one of the trucks took the wheel of our bus for the remainder of the run into the next town. Yep, as always the show rolls on, again and again.

We found out afterwards that Mac was a Valium addict. He took them every night for his "nerves." No wonder his driving always sucked, but who would suspect such a thing? It is absolutely dumbfounding how flunkies like this can slip through the cracks in any industry and wind up at the professional levels, but they do sometimes. In my opinion, there should have been charges brought. Mac should have gone to jail and lost his CDL for good so nobody else could ever be put at the same risk again, but it's the music business and there never seems to be the time or the will to rectify problems the right way with so much pressure to stay on schedule.

From Buddy Holly to Lynyrd Skynyrd to Reba McIntyre's band, that pressure has been a big factor in so many people in this trade tragically losing their lives on the road. Even though old Mac got sent home right afterwards, we heard later he was still driving a coach on gambling junkets down in Mississippi.

Go figure.

It wasn't our day to die, but it probably would have been if not for quick thinking by Joey and Griff and their heroic actions. Sometimes people don't know what the term "Road Warrior" really means.

Had this been a military outfit, I would have done all I could to see them have medals pinned on their chests. Joey and Griff, thank you for saving my life and the lives of eleven other people.

God bless you, wherever you are.

CHAPTER 24

Mother's Day

December 1995

I got a call at my home one evening from my mother. She sounded upbeat and chipper as always, but I could tell something wasn't quite right. We caught up on everyday stuff for a bit, but then an awkward silence fell over the phone line.

"Is everything okay, Mom?" I asked.

She replied, "Well, there are some things we need to discuss, but I would like to talk to you in person if your schedule allows, my dear." When I was growing up, she always used "my dear" either before bringing up a serious matter, or afterward to make a point—a "keyword" that always got my attention. This keyword caught my attention now, and I felt a stab of cold dread in my gut. She had not been in the best of health lately.

"We are pretty slow right now, Mom. I can come down in a couple of days," I said.

It was a day's drive to where she and my father lived on Pawley's Island, South Carolina.

A few days later, I walked into their house to a warm greeting. Ever the hostess, my mother had happy hour arranged with a pitcher of Bloody Marys in the blender and cheese and crackers laid out.

My parents and I sat around the bar for a little while, just chatting and catching up. My dad excused himself to the garage to tinker with something, leaving my mother and me alone. When the screen door to the garage slammed shut, she cut to the chase.

"I had some tests done recently. They found cancer in my left lung. It has metastasized badly. I have terminal bone cancer, Mark. I have about four months."

I stared at her while everything in the room seemed to fade away. There in the center of my vision her piercing blue eyes stared back at me. We each held the gaze for a long time, communicating only the way soulmates can. Without a word, she held me there in her eyes, imploring me to recall what she had raised me to remember at times like these. Her sayings reverberated in my ears, now suddenly ringing a little more than usual. *"All separations are only temporary."*

"When I pass someday, son, if you cry and mope like a two-year-old, I swear I will come back and haunt you. Live on! We have it backwards in this culture. We should cry when a baby is born and celebrate when an old person dies. Never, ever, ever show grief in public; it makes others uncomfortable."

She was a very dignified woman of the old school.

"Why the hell do people spend ten-thousand dollars on a cheesy show to put five bucks worth of chemicals in the ground?" she would say. That was one of my favorites.

"Mother's Day? Paah! Every day should be Mother's Day!" That was one of her favorites.

We sat there for a long time, not saying anything.

Then I stood up, put my arms around her, and said, "I'm here. I love you, and I will do anything you need me to do." I held her closely and noticed how frail her body had already become. My "stick of dynamite" mother felt like an armful of dry fall leaves.

"Well, for now you can pour me another one of those Bloody Marys!" she said with a wink. The gallows humor eased the lump in my throat, and we both laughed.

That was my mother. She hated anything sappy. She hated sympathy from others, yet she was always the first to sympathize with them.

She finished her Bloody Mary, then held her head high, got up, straightened up the kitchen, and called out to my father in the garage: "John, let's go, dear. We will be late."

With that, we all piled into the car and headed down to a restaurant owned by some friends. We enjoyed a wonderful evening of laughter, drinks, good food, and great company.

The next day, I wanted to stay a few more days to help with anything they might need.

"No, no, my dear, you have a family at home. Your place is there for them. You run along; we are all set. Call when you get in."

Still numb from the news, I decided to process everything once I got home. There she was, dying of cancer, but sounding like I was twelve again, gently admonishing me for not paying proper attention to "more important things."

God, she was awesome.

The doctors did their best to get her to submit to an exhaustive treatment schedule. She would have none of it. At one time, they said she only had half the time left that they originally thought, and if she would just try some of the medication, she might have more time.

When I asked why she wouldn't try it, she said, "That's a bunch of rubbish, Mark. It's all just about money. I will go when my time comes. I will die in my own home, and I will go with dignity."

I knew better than to argue.

My mother died five months later. She lived an extra month just to prove the doctors wrong, I think.

She left this world on Thursday evening, May 8, 1996, on her mother's birthday. In her final hours, I sat with her on the edge of the bed in her room. She could no longer speak, but I've been told the terminally ill can still hear even in the last stages.

I just talked about how things were going in my world at the time. I felt like it was what she wanted to hear. After all, I believe she was somebody who could have been a true star in her own right, had she stayed on Broadway so long ago. She had lived the unrealized dreams of her youth vicariously through me for many years. I'm so glad she got to see the big time in that way.

It took the nurse about three hours to gather her things and prepare my mother's body for the final exit from the house. Just before they carried her out, I went into her room to say one last good-bye. I stroked her head, bidding her farewell. As I turned to go, I placed my hand over her heart. Long, long after her body had ceased to function and the chill of death had overtaken it, the place where that heart had so vibrantly beaten for seventy-six years was shockingly warm. All her days, she loved life and lived it with unbridled passion. I guess the fire from that passion just refused to go out quickly. The warmth in her chest seemed as if she were still lingering, trying to send my father and me one last comfort.

The following day, the band had a show in Myrtle Beach. I was in Pawley's Island, only about thirty miles south of there. Late Thursday night, after Mother passed, I felt like my father needed some time alone; so I left and drove up to my hotel in Myrtle Beach. It was a long, long night, and I got no rest. I suppose I could have called and asked the rest of the guys to cancel the show, but that was the last thing I ever would have done, considering how my mother was. She would have been disgusted.

At the venue, I kept myself compartmentalized and focused. Despite the surrealistic day before, I managed to hold my emotions at bay because that's how I was taught. I am so thankful for that. It was a special show that night—lots of families in the crowd. Of all things, it was Mother's Day weekend.

As the house lights went down and I walked toward the drum riser, I felt like I was floating. Again, everything came into super-sharp focus. As I started to play, I felt empowerment like I had never felt before. My hands and feet articulated things that I didn't think I was capable of—without even trying. Magic infused the stage, and I think everyone felt it.

As the sweat poured and the machines belched smoke around the drum riser,

I felt a presence behind me. Thinking it my drum tech tweaking something that needed a fix, I turned around to see. It was very hot under those lights, and I had very little sleep, and I know the mind can do funny things under stress, but I swear I saw my mother on that riser with me. Her face lit up in the biggest smile I'd ever seen. She somehow communicated to me that she was so happy. A million things were just perfect wherever her spirit now resided. Even over the volume of the music, I heard her voice in my head. "Thank you for tonight, son. I am so proud *of* you and *for* you. You will be fine—always."

I shook my head, turned to look again, and found only the lingering smoke effects and an empty riser.

The joy and peace I felt that night is never fleeting. I can still feel it when I need to. Thank you, Mother, for who you were and still are to me. You were the first one to teach me, "The show goes on . . .

"Now . . . go break a leg."

CHAPTER 25

A Torch Is Passed

And you, my father, there on the sad height . . .
Do not go gentle into that good night.
Rage, rage against the dying of the light.

Dylan Thomas (1947)

*   *   *

Two years after my mother passed, my dad was diagnosed with an aortic aneurism.

After her death, he really didn't know what to do with himself. For the most part, he lived a listless, day-to-day existence. I think he fell into the "Neal Armstrong Syndrome." That happens to people sometimes when they have reached all their goals and there doesn't seem to be anything left worth striving for. Some days, I can relate a little bit, but I fight it.

Dad went in for major surgery to correct the problem, but the procedure was bungled somehow. His brain had become damaged due to insufficient oxygen, which I blame on the anesthesiologist. It was something I couldn't prove, but had plenty of reason to believe, my dad came out of it a semi-vegetable. The man I knew growing up, twelve feet tall and bigger than John Wayne, lay helpless and trapped in a hospital bed, tethered to feeding tubes and a ventilator—one of life's cruelties.

I was heartbroken for him, and he was totally disgusted and embarrassed. I had him flown to Chattanooga to a hospital there to begin therapy in hopes of having him closer to us. With family closer by, I hoped it would better his chances to get off the ventilator.

Being on a ventilator is hell on Earth for the patient. He was flat on his back 24/7, mouth agape, with a breathing tube rammed down his throat. He couldn't eat; he couldn't swallow; he couldn't sleep. He developed a nasty condition in his mouth called "thrush," where germs turn it into a petri dish, cultivating all kinds of infectious bacteria. A man who was active all his life had to lie there immobile for hours at a time, totally dependent on the nursing staff for basic care. How humiliating that must have been.

He lived like that for 130 days.

I wanted so much for him to get well so he could move closer to us, so he could to get to know my daughter—his granddaughter—and most of all so she could get to know him. It was very frustrating. He was unable to speak since the original surgery.

I was on the road and could only visit him occasionally. The prognosis never got any better. I came back for a visit one day in late August 1998 after a long run out to the West Coast.

I came directly from the airport to the hospital where my wife, Karen, sat in the room with him. She was closer to him in many ways than I. They had really grown to like one another. She spent a lot of time with him in that room as the weeks turned into months, keeping him company, watching TV, reading to him, and just being there. It was pretty special. When I walked in, his face lit up, but he couldn't talk, so he just smiled and stared at me. I felt like he was yearning to tell me something. We stayed for another hour.

Karen and I had to head back to Fort Payne to pick up our daughter. He knew we were leaving. He closed his eyes, and a look of sadness and resignation came over his square-jawed face—something I'd never seen before.

Karen left the room to go get the car.

His eyes still closed, I put my hand on his forehead and said, "Dad, I want you to know I love you very much. You are one hell of a man's man. I wish I could have been more like you in so many ways."

I had read somewhere that people in terminal stages sometimes want "permission" from their loved ones to go on if there's no hope; they don't want to burden us with their troubles. Even though Dad's condition was no burden, by any stretch, I could empathize with that. I would be the same way if I were that sick.

Thinking of how he must have felt lying there helplessly, I continued, "Thank you for looking after my girls while I was gone. I'm here now. I've got them and a change of command has been authorized."

His expression went from troubled to peaceful.

"You know, Dad, this ain't no life for a guy like you. If you want to go, go. Go see Mom and tell her everything is all right. I am so proud you are my father. It's okay. It's really okay." I patted him on the shoulder, reached down and kissed his forehead, and left, thinking I would still see him in a day or two.

Not fifteen minutes down the road toward home, the cellphone rang, someone from the hospital. "I am sorry to inform you that Colonel Herndon has just passed."

My dad, even though bedridden, was not going to leave his post guarding my family until a proper replacement arrived to relieve him. In his mind, he was going to serve for something until the end—once a Marine, always a Marine.

A month later, I called down to Fort Payne airport and rented a small single-engine plane. I took off that chilly September afternoon with a very special passenger aboard—the ashes of Colonel John L. "Bull" Herndon, USMC (Ret) were to go aloft one last time.

As I climbed away from the earthly bonds, a total peace came over me. I climbed on toward the broken overcast, the sun's rays stabbing through holes like golden swords thrust from heaven, slanting into the earth below. I looked over at the urn in the seat beside me and smiled.

"Wonder what the poor folks are doing today, Dad?" I said to the otherwise empty cockpit.

The engine purring out front and pulling me ever higher, I punched through an opening in the cloud base and flew into brilliant sunshine with a snow-white cloud deck falling away below. It was as if one door had closed, leaving my concerns of the world behind, and another one opened, allowing me—or at least this flight anyway—to be where I belonged on that day with someone who had *always* belonged there. I imagined a circle of ghost planes piloted by long-gone brothers-in-arms circling high above me, waiting for their old friend to join them. With no clouds above me, the higher I flew, the more beautiful the sky became.

Aircraft piston engines for the most part are like people. After reaching a certain height, they don't get enough oxygen in thin air to provide sufficient performance. After climbing as high as I possibly could, I leveled off. There, I just cruised around, reflecting on all that had come to pass in my years knowing my father, and all that must have passed in the life of the man whose remains now sat waiting for me to complete my mission.

I opened the urn, then I opened the window. I said, "Blue skies and tailwinds, Colonel," and poured the contents out into the slipstream. The freezing wind took them over the tail wing in a brief white wisp, gone in a split second, disappearing into the vastness. I shut the window and turned my face upward in the windshield and said, "Goodbye, Dad. Look for me on your wing someday." I threw up a salute, pushed the nose over, and built up some speed.

Going fast now, I eased the nose back up through the horizon and applied full left aileron. The earth and sky swapped places as my little craft did a victory roll for my father. It was a proper send-off for an extraordinary man.

Rolling wings level—knowing my dad was finally free at last—I started back down the long descent for the airport with my earthly concerns waiting to reclaim me.

Two weeks later, I was returning home after picking up my third-grade daughter from school. She had been very quiet the whole ride home. Up until this point, she hadn't had much to say about my father's passing, nor had she spoken much about "Nomie," her pet name for my mom. Thinking she might have had a bad day, I kept mum, just letting her decompress for a little bit.

As we turned into the driveway, she reached over and placed her little hand on my arm. In all seriousness, she said, "I'm sorry about your dad, Dad." She looked out the window for a moment and resumed. "It's going to be okay, though. Right now, Pawz and Nomie are in a big room. There is a stage with curtains, and chairs all set up in front. He is sitting in one of those chairs. He is all by himself. He has his dress uniform on with a sword. She is going to come out on that stage in her ballerina dress and she will dance for him. He will get up and go to the stage; he'll climb the stairs and she will take his hand. They will walk off toward the back of the stage and they will go on up."

She stared at me as though this were the Word, and I should not to question it.

I didn't.

Satisfied that she had made her point, she nodded her head, waiting while I parked. She smiled at me, patted my arm, and said, "Okay, let's go jump on the trampoline!"

With that, she was out the door, singing, little feet carrying her to play after school like any other day. I sat there for a long time, watching her. I couldn't show her the tears of joy she had given me. I didn't want her to think the beautiful thing she said was somehow wrong.

I watched her bounce like Tigger on that trampoline, realizing the best part of both my parents were very much still here and always would be, in that little, but oh-so-big heart of my daughter.

CHAPTER 26

Karma

Out there in the spotlight you're a million miles away
Every ounce of energy you try to give away
As the sweat pours out your body like the music that you play

"Turn the Page" Bob Seger

*   *   *

Five years after I was thrown out of a Doobie Brothers concert, five years after I promised myself I would perform at the Carolina Coliseum, it came true. After five years of riding the rocket to the top of the charts, my band performed one night on the very same stage where I once watched in hunger from the rafter seats.

We played to a sold-out house of our own. It was indescribable; the crowd completely drowned out the PA system. We played five encores, and on one we had to stop playing and just let them scream. At first, it was sort of funny, and that drove people to cheer even louder. Then, it got really emotional because everyone suddenly realized we were all making history together.

Something very special happened in that room that evening, and tears started to flow. When we started playing again, it was a snapshot of heaven. Even the security personnel and cops got into it. No wrong existed in the world—no hate, no jealousy, no bad. Band and crowd were of one mind and spirit that night. The synergy, from the stage all the way to those rafter seats, overpowered every soul in that space. Memories like these are priceless; I hold on to them with reverence—little pearls planted in my spirit forever.

They keep me going, sometimes.

It wasn't just the energy from the people that intoxicated, but what I was feeling from within the building, too. I know that sounds silly, but it seemed real to me. Before we launched buses and trucks for another town, I found my way in the dark back outside to a spot where I put my hand on the wall of that hallowed venue so long ago. I looked up and whispered to nobody in particular, "Told you so."

I felt like she heard me and smiled.

Now mid-summer 1987, I had been with the band for nine years. We had just begun a two-and-a-half-year tour with The Charlie Daniels Band, starting off in Pittsburgh, Pennsylvania, downtown at the Coliseum. Opening night of the tour, it had sold out to the roof—*the* hot-ticket event in town that night.

Just about an hour before showtime, warming up on my practice pads in the dressing room, I thought about trying to go down and meet one of my long-time idols: Charlie Daniels. *Why not? Hell, we're in this together; would be nice to strike up a friendship or two.*

I went and knocked on the CDB dressing-room door. I introduced myself and asked if I could meet some of the guys.

"Come on in, man," said the guy at the door. "Big fan of you guys."

The hospitality was so gracious and humble. The whole band was just hanging out, pickin' on guitars, or just chillin'. I felt at ease right off.

Taz (R.I.P., bro), the keyboard player, got me a beer. "Have a seat, man. We are so excited about this tour!"

Toasts went all around and, before long, we were all chatting, laughing, and swapping road stories. It felt as if I had been with these guys for the past nine years instead of the other band.

I just had to tell the story about my first time seeing them perform way back when at Francis Marion College. I was on a roll, embellishing my story with all the freaky stuff, and finally got to the part about me sneaking in like a student worker.

Then I noticed Charlie got really quiet. He pulled his trademark ten-gallon cowboy hat down over his shades and just listened. "That's a great story, son," he said. "You know, I think I actually remember playing that venue."

Now about ten minutes before they were to go on, I figured that was my cue to leave them alone for some private time. I walked over to Charlie and said, "It's such an honor to finally meet you, man."

He just nodded and said, "'Preciate it, son. Have a good show."

I told Taz the next beer was on me. We shook hands all around, and I left.

The next week or so, the pace proved unbelievable. We didn't have much time for socializing because of the logistical kinks we had to work out—starting out a new tour between crews, dealing with so much equipment, distance between shows, meet-and-greet with radio folks and fans, etc.

One night, about two weeks into the tour, after the daily routines and rhythms started to take care of themselves, I was summoned from my dressing room to Charlie's room by a huge burly, mean-ass looking stagehand. "Charlie wants to see you, pronto," was all he said as he jerked his thumb in the general direction of the CDB dressing room.

The guy followed me down the hall, opened the door, came in with me, locked it, and stood behind me. Gone was the friendly atmosphere of before. No other band members were present. Charlie was seated at a foldout table covered with lots of paperwork, pens and pencils, and an adding machine spewing about ten feet of curly paper down to the floor. Seated around the table were Charlie's business manager, road manager and tour accountant. Three other rough-looking security types stood back a little way from the table, looking as if they had just finished up a nice meal of ten-penny nails.

Silence. The room was quiet as a tomb.

"Have a seat, Mr. Herndon," said the road manager at last. I pulled the metal folding chair back and dragged it across the tile floor. The scratching noise made me cringe. Something was up and it was bad.

I sat down. Still, not a word was said for about five more long minutes as the accountant finished clicking away furiously on his adding machine. I sat there feeling all eyes hard upon me. No one was smiling.

I looked up at Charlie. He had that hat pulled down over his eyes, arms folded, wearing a serious expression.

"Mr. Herndon," Charlie began, "the story you related about the show at Francis Marion College, on September 28, 1977, has been brought to the attention of our general accounting office."

"Okay," I said, wondering what he was talking about.

He continued. "The general admission ticket price for that show back then was fifteen dollars. With that as a figure to start from, plus adding amortization and compounded interest on said price, it is by our calculations that you, sir, owe CDB Touring Inc. the sum of . . ."

He adjusted his reading glasses, looked down at his work again, and continued.

"One thousand eight hundred seventy-nine dollars and forty-seven cents." He pushed the official invoice across the table and sat back with a "Whatcha gonna do about it, little fella?" look on his face.

The business manager then chimed in. "We can take cash or check; it's up to you." I looked at the invoice on official letterhead.

Stunned, I looked at Charlie, who was now stone-faced like all the others. I felt like I had gotten myself into some serious shit, like maybe these guys operate like the Mafia or something. "I'll have to write you a check, if that's all right," I said meekly.

The stone faces sat there for about ten more seconds, and then . . .

Charlie busts out laughing.

All the other band members came into the dressing room from another entrance, laughing, too.

Charlie stretched his hand out across the table and said, "Aw hell, we was just playing with ya, son. Welcome to the family! You were the only one that came down and introduced yourself the other night. We thought that was kind of cool since y'all are such a big name now, so we just wanted to have a li'l fun!"

It had been a wind-up! Much relieved, I busted out laughing with them—and at myself for having been had so easily.

Beers and cheers worked their way around the table. I went back to my dressing room, my laughter echoing in the hallway.

From that day forward, we forged friendships that have lasted a lifetime. The bonds you develop with people who share the same passions, hardships, and glory with you are sometimes almost stronger than blood family.

Things come back to you in this business. In the late 1990s, we did a show at the Alabama Theatre. Ed Turbeville, my old boss with the top-forty variety band, came with his wife, Mary, and Sally, my old friend from the early days. Ed could barely get around these days, but undaunted, he made the effort to come down from Florence for the show.

I got them front row seats. It was one of those rare nights where everything about the show came off perfectly; we all had our game on. I played my ass off to a packed house that night. Afterward, we went backstage. Sally and Mary were teary-eyed, and old Ed was grinning like a bird-fed cat.

We sat in the Green Room—what all backstage hospitality rooms are called—for a long time after the show. Some of my friends on the road crew were hanging out with us. It came my turn to share some wild stories, and I did.

But, not to be outdone, Ed held everyone's rapt attention telling a few on me. Everybody just kept laughing. It was great.

When the party began to die down and it was time to go, Ed, Mary, and Sally gave me a bear hug. Now in his late eighties and still sporting jet-black-dyed hair, Ed pulled me aside and said in his deep South Carolina drawl, "Maaahk. You little shit. Ah always knew this would happen for you someday. Ah just knew it deep down. A'hm so glad Ah have lived to see it. You play so good. Solid as a brick, just like we used to talk about, remembah? Ah'm so damn proud." I think he felt like he had a part in seeing me make it.

Well, Ed, I think you did, too.

CHAPTER 27

Jammin' in June

The "June Jam" was a charity concert held every year for sixteen straight years throughout the 1980s and '90s—the stuff of local legend around Ft. Payne, Alabama. From a small start at the high-school football field, the concert grew into a world-renowned event. It got so big, it took on a life of its own—well, apart from the band. June Jam raised millions of dollars for local and national charities alike.

We had folks pitching in to help with everything. It would have been impossible to pull off every year if it weren't for the volunteers doing much of the grunt work that makes or breaks a show. Thanks go out to the state troopers, sheriffs' deputies, police, and fire departments of DeKalb County. Thanks to the EMTs and rescue squads for going above and beyond all those years in the hot sun. Thanks to the countless locals who donated days and weeks of their time to help with thousands of logistical nightmares—which are always a part of big outdoor shows.

The planning was so labor intensive that usually show day would mark the beginning of preparing for next year's event. I used to tell people it was like painting the Golden Gate Bridge. From what I hear, by the time a crew would finish painting, it was time to start again at the other end.

There are so many stories attached to the phenomenon of June Jam. I think someone could write another book about just that. The culmination of a year's planning would end up with more than a hundred-thousand people descending on little Ft. Payne, Alabama, a town with only about 10,000 residents back then.

It was a lot to ask of such a small town, but the community rose to the occasion year after year with a welcoming spirit I have yet to witness anywhere else.

DeKalb County was "dry" back then; no alcohol sales were permitted by law. The next county over was "wet," so anybody who wanted to wet their whistle just drove to the county line to get adult beverages. With the town lying amongst the foothills of the Appalachian Mountains, plenty of good moonshine could always be had—if you knew the right folks. I used to say that DeKalb County was dry for 364 days a year. On the June Jam show day, it was "damp," to say the least.

Some people thought we were crazy for having the event in a dry county in the first place. Maybe we were, but it never seemed to deter the fans from coming. From hitchhiking to flying, they came from all over the world; we had folks from England, across Europe, and as far away as Japan.

Now, the Jam staff tried to honor the local laws as best they could, but you just can't keep a close eye on that many people all at once. People would find ingenious ways to bring alcohol and other contraband into the shows. They'd hide stuff in false-bottomed coolers, children's toys, soft drink bottles, mattresses . . . You name it; the gatekeepers saw it all.

I found a way to bring it in, too, but in a different way. Backstage was always quite the party atmosphere. It was a chance to visit and hang out with all the other big-named acts that would come to play. Sometimes, folks would want to enjoy a cocktail before their performances and, naturally, after. It's just the way showbiz is.

After a long day in the sun, a lot of the volunteers would want a cold one, too. I thought they deserved it and, of course, I wanted some on hand for myself. In those days, only one way led to the June Jam site, a two-lane road that, for several days, became nearly impassable because of the traffic.

We hired the services of a helicopter outfit from Birmingham. The talent that didn't come in on a bus would fly into Ft. Payne Airport or park off-site about 10 miles away. The helicopters would ferry people in, to and from, and run errands that were nearly impossible due to the clogged roadway.

One year in particular, I remember we ran out of the hospitality beer stash backstage. I had made friends with the helo pilots, even tried my hand flying one of the birds every now and then when the pilot had the jump seat open.

I was quite the beer drinker and hellraiser those days. Knowing the situation, and feeling obligated to do something about it, I went to one of the pilots with my idea.

"Jim," I said, "I got a little detour in mind for the next time you come back empty."

Probably tired of the same routing back and forth all day, he brightened and asked,

"Sure, what's up?"

"Wanna run into Cambodia for some supplies?" I asked with a wink.

He knew right then what I was referring to, so he smiled and said, "Hop in!"

I jumped into the seat, strapped in, and donned my headset.

Jim pulled pitch and we rose off the sweltering landing zone. We headed northeast, away from the sea of humanity below. With the front doors removed from the helicopter, the 100-knot wind streaming in felt refreshing. I knew exactly where a bootlegger lived; I gave Jim directions as we flew.

The bootlegger sold beer, wine, and moonshine out of the back of his house. I had been there many times before via my own transportation; he knew me, and he knew my car. What he didn't know, at the time, was one of his loyal customers was coming to call—by air.

I had Jim follow the road up to his very small rural house situated way back in the woods. We flew overhead and picked out a landing spot in a clearing about 75 yards from his back porch. Jim flew around the spot a couple of times, making sure it was safe. This helicopter was a turbine powered Bell Jet Ranger, meaning noisy enough to draw lots of attention.

The bootlegger's house was miles away from anywhere, so you can imagine how the peace and quiet must have been shattered by our sudden presence overhead. Jim began the final descent to land in the clearing, and I prepared to get out. I was gonna walk up to the back door and surprise him.

But, I'm the one who got the surprise.

Once we touched down, I unfastened my lap belt and started to step out of the helicopter—

"Uh-oh," Jim said over the headset.

I looked up to see the bootlegger with an M-16 raised shoulder high, marching right toward us.

He wasn't happy.

Trying to yell over the sound of screaming jet engine just two feet from my head proved futile. So, I did the only thing I could think of. Anticipating the searing pain of hot lead striking my body at any second, I raised my hands in the air with a wad of money in one hand and the other with palm wide open.

The guy stopped his march toward us, lowered his weapon a bit, and stood there peering at me. I pantomimed a drinking motion, then took off my ball cap and mimicked playing the drums while pointing at myself. He slowly began to process what I was trying to tell him. He motioned for me to come closer.

We laughed as he told me he thought we were "gubmint men" coming to get him.

I didn't laugh when I realized how serious he was about protecting his property. Folks back in these parts, a lot of them, are a throwback to the old days of Appalachia, when people lived and survived by their own laws, minded their own business, and the rest of the world be damned. *Very American*, if you ask me.

Whatever anxiety we had caused the old guy was forgotten. My bootlegger friend made a tidy profit that day, and we parted company with a back slap and a handshake. With beer loaded and passenger secured, the pilot throttled up, pulled pitch, and headed back into the present, back to the show site, with hardscrabble reality receding behind us.

Mission accomplished—spirits delivered.

I never said anything to anyone about my little trip to "Cambodia." No one asked, and everyone was just grateful for the refreshments.

I ran into Jim about fifteen years later. He became an FAA examiner, and I had been working on my helicopter rating for about a year. After I passed the check ride, we had some laughs about that day long ago.

DeKalb County eventually became "wet"—which just about put all the bootleggers out of business—another storied American tradition gone in the name of progress.

The June Jam faded into history. It's only a grassy field now.

A whole new generation of people drive by that site every day with no idea of the extraordinary events that took place there for so many years. Many would consider that field unremarkable, but some of us once saw it covered with stages, screens, lights, buses, trucks, and big tents, the air reverberating, music echoing off the mountains, the night sky ripped open by huge fireworks. More than a million souls over a 16-year span enjoyed the privilege of experiencing the June Jam.

It did some good for some good causes. Many around the area don't have any idea that the schools their kids attend now are some of the best in the state largely due to June Jam.

It was fun, and for a time, it brought people from all walks of life together in a wonderful small-town-America way. The way it was.

The way I wish it could always be.

CHAPTER 28

Ch-Ch-Ch-Changes

Early in the morning on February 20, 1989—5:32AM, to be exact—my daughter, Katie, came into the world. The doctor gently lifted a little pink cherub from my wife's abdomen; she was delivered C-section. Katie was red-faced, screaming, mad as hell, and peeing all over everybody.

I stood there in my surgical garb, watching in total awe.

It seemed like she was struggling to get away from all the hands trying to clean her off and suction her mouth. She didn't have time for that! She was here. And she wanted to get on with it!

One of the nurses took her over to weigh her, and the doc said to me, "You've got a good one there, Mark. When they come out with a big fuss like that, it's a really good sign. Healthy and strong-willed."

I was glad for the mask covering my face; it absorbed the tears of absolute joy that streamed from my eyes. I said, "Yeah, and probably stubborn like her old man, too."

Everybody laughed.

Because of the C-section, my wife, Karen, was sedated and unconscious; the nurse handed the baby to me. I so wished she was conscious so we could have met our daughter together, but this would have to do for now. Almost twenty-six years later, I can still feel that bundle of life in my arms for the first time—cradling her closely as I spoke softly to her.

Here was a brand new being, a new soul . . . a gift fresh from heaven. I felt as close to this being as any mortal man could in this lifetime.

The change in my life happened instantly. I felt an overpowering, uncondi-tional, instant love. I felt complete. I felt an animal-like fierceness in wanting to protect this beautiful innocent life against anything that could do her harm.

Her cries abated to a soft whimpering as she nestled her little head against my chest. I was so happy. I just held her and held her. My soul smiled. She stopped whimpering and fell asleep.

The nurse came up to me and said, "We have to run some tests, just the routine stuff. I will give her back as soon as we're done; I promise." I didn't want to let go of my new baby girl. It was rough, but after some coaxing, I finally gave in.

"You will have to walk her down the aisle someday, Mark. It won't get any easier," said the doctor. I put *that* outta my mind immediately.

After the tests were done, Katie and I spent the next four hours just walking up and down the hall of the maternity ward. Karen was just beginning to come out of anesthesia. At last, she got to hold our baby. It was another teary, joyful moment for me—and for her, too.

Karen settled into the room to recuperate, and the nurse brought Katie in to her mom for some bonding time. I had been in the hospital most of the day, not at all enjoying the food, so I felt a little cooped up. I wanted to get out and shout to the world about my new kid.

Karen was in a lot of pain; she was going to have to stay an extra day. For the most part, everything seemed okay. So, I headed back home to get a change of clothes and gather some things we needed.

On the way, since I hadn't really eaten much in the past 24 hours, I stopped at a seafood restaurant to get a good meal.

I remember it was some kind of a shrimp dish. It smelled a little funny, but I was ravenous and, over the years on the road, I had developed an iron gut. So, I didn't heed the warning. I gulped it down and drove home.

I hadn't been home for more than thirty minutes when the phone rang. It was Karen's obstetrician. "Mark, you need to get back down here as soon as you can. Karen is experiencing some problems." Not what a husband or a new dad wants to hear.

"What's the matter?" I asked.

"Just hurry," was all he said.

Speeding tickets be damned, I rushed back down the hill and drove through town like a madman. With flashers blinking, I darted around slowpokes and ran red lights.

Right after I left the hospital, Karen had gone into some sort of seizure. Her heart had nearly stopped beating. Unbeknownst to anyone at the time, Karen was bleeding dangerously internally.

As I walked into the room, the medical team had just managed to stabilize her with a fourth unit of blood. She was white as a ghost, but the readouts on the machine behind her were now showing positive heart rate and blood pressure. The doctor said she had hemorrhaged badly after they closed her up.

No one knew what to do except him. He had seen this condition before. He happened to be making rounds that evening and recognized the signs. An emergency procedure was done on the spot and the units of blood saved her life. The doctor told me later that I came very close to becoming a single parent that day.

Karen wasn't going home for a few days, so I got a cot to sleep on. I sat down—exhausted. I began to get dizzy, and a little nausea feeling fluttered in my stomach. I went to the nurse's station down the hall and asked for something to make me feel better. The nurse gave me some Phenergan orally. As time ticked, I became sicker and sicker. Before long, I was evacuating from both ends at the same time.

Ahhh, what a pair we were in that hospital!—a brand new baby and *both* parents incapacitated!

At shift change a new nurse came in to check on Karen, who was feeling somewhat better. I was lying on the bathroom floor, moaning and covered in excrement of various kinds. The nurse got more Phenergan, but because of the shift change, the new staffer wasn't aware of my previous maximum dose ingested just an hour before.

Since I couldn't swallow anything, I received the Phenergan from a needle this time. The food-poisoning symptoms got worse—elevated now by a fever.

A doctor was summoned, and he had me taken to X-ray. On the way down, the double dose of Phenergan kicked in, and now I was hallucinating.

I saw the doctors through a doorway at the end of a hallway. They were standing around an operating table. I could see their mouths grinning at me through their surgical masks. They sharpened their scalpels in anticipation of my arrival, then just laughed.

I was strapped on a gurney and tried to get off, yelling at the orderlies to let me go. It was like a scene right out of a horror movie—and the way patients in mental hospitals used to be treated.

The doctors, the orderlies—everybody was in on the dark secret of what they were about to do to me. Everyone knew except me . . .

And just as the foot of the gurney pushed open the door where doctors poised with their scalpels held high in the air for the final plunge into my flesh . . . I mercifully passed out.

I don't remember anything except waking up the next morning in my own room across the hall from Karen on the maternity ward—the only male ever to be admitted there. As I recuperated, the nurse told me they had no vacancies on the other floors, so they were keeping me for observation. After what I thought I saw and caterwauled to the orderlies about, I figured a shrink was probably doing the observation.

Karen was on the mend, and I was fine the next day. The doc said the miscommunication on the Phenergan caused an overdose. Others said it was stress from the previous day. I say I'm glad I've never tried LSD! If LSD takes you further out than Phenergan does, I don't think I would ever make it back.

The next two decades blessed Karen and me with a wonderful home in which to raise a child. We lived in Mentone, Alabama, high atop Lookout Mountain. Katie spent all of her formative years there. She attended public school the first six years where the entire student body numbered fewer than 200 kids. We were accepted in a small town—just how I like it. No special treatment—no special attention.

Katie learned early on that my job did not grant her any privilege. As she grew, I was lucky enough to enjoy some time off between tour dates to spend with her.

In my own childhood, I never got to know my dad as closely as I wanted. I admired, feared, and loved him, but we just never got to do many things together. My dad's line of work took him away from family just as much as mine. I was determined not to let that happen to my daughter and me.

From toddler to twenty, we did everything we could together. We camped, we fished, we skied, we swam, and we flew. I loved doing homework with Katie at night where she would *teach me* how to do fractions, or spell the day's vocabulary words. I played dumb to her delight. I didn't have to play too hard, and I still can't do algebra.

I drove out of the driveway of my home many a time feeling like my heart was breaking, having to leave again and again. It was hard for Katie at first, but she soon got used to the rhythm of our lifestyle.

As she grew, I was able to start taking her on trips to places like New York, Los Angeles, Boston, and Montreal. Traditional small town values are a priceless base, but I wanted her to discover a big and very interesting world out there. I am lucky to have been able to do that. I started letting her ride the bus on short trips. The crew guys loved having her aboard because I was really stern about manners and bus etiquette. It paid off for her many ways in later years. I could go on forever because I am so proud of my daughter, but I won't.

During Katie's youth, with the exception of usual adolescent quirks, Karen and I felt like the luckiest parents on earth. Watching a child grow up successfully in an idyllic setting, and benefiting from it, is one of the greatest satisfactions in life.

Amidst the indescribable blessings that a child can bring lurks the reality that the child will also leave you someday. When a child is born, it is a major life change; when she or he leaves, it's a major life change.

As any good parents are supposed to do, we encouraged our daughter to find her own way in the world, to enable her to eventually leave the nest on her own. Katie did, and she did it well.

As our beloved daughter grew up, Karen and I began to grow apart.

After that last final show, the touring days came to an end for me. Suddenly we had a lot less money coming in, and we both had to throw ourselves into our jobs to make ends meet. Out of necessity, Karen took a full time job in Gadsden, Alabama, as a hospital administrator; I went to work as a pilot for a large company in Ft. Payne.

Over the following years, we gradually became more like roommates than a loving married couple. The lack of quality time is a ticking time bomb in any relationship. We saw some things change, and we saw some that wouldn't.

The nest now empty, and with us both focused in different directions, we no longer found the common ground to keep us close. With the distance growing wider, and neither of us having the desire or time to bridge that gap, we ran out of gas and finally hit the wall.

Karen and I divorced after twenty-plus years, and we went our separate ways. We were two very strong-willed individuals who, as we became older, grew to become two entirely different people.

The decision was the best for the both of us, if either of us were ever to be happy again. Karen and I remain friends, and we wish one another the very best for success and happiness moving forward. If all divorces were as drama-free as ours, lawyers would starve.

In the meantime, Katie has grown to become a fine young woman. She's a college graduate married to a good hardworking young man.

Katie was an exceptional child growing up. Wise beyond her years, she just naturally avoided those things that might lead her down the wrong path.

Yeah, Karen and I were good parents, dedicating our lives to raising the best kid possible, but I feel like Katie raised herself. She was an adult of sorts early on.

I am not naïve; all kids get into some mischief—and she is a Herndon, after all—but overall, she has paid her mother and me back with honor, responsibility, determination, courage, initiative, conscientiousness, and love.

Katie and I still share that same bond that we built walking the hospital floor all those years ago with her in my arms, wrapped in a blanket, a tiny sock on her precious, little pink head.

CHAPTER 29

Last Chance

Life on the road can be hard—an understatement of *grand* proportions! Although wonderfully satisfying at times, being a "road warrior" is stressful and full of temptations not always found in a more domestic lifestyle. Being away from home, one becomes debased from societal norms. I lived hard for many years, never missing an opportunity to ride on the wild side. For a long time, I pushed the limits in everything I did, including my health. My behavior crept into the realm of self-destruction sooner than I wanted to admit. I could always look toward another town to start fresh, a new shore to run to, whenever I felt it all catching up to me.

Eventually, the time came when something had to give, and boy, did it! At the time, it didn't feel like one, but it came in the form of a gift.

On April 22, 2004, I quit drinking and partying forever. After an all-nighter on the bus, I attempted to drive myself home early that morning. I had no business behind the wheel, but years of cheating the hangman made me think I could do it like I had *so* many times before—the kind of foolish mistake that all too often winds up tragically for so many unfortunate souls.

Stepping off the bus into the unwelcoming bright morning light, I stumbled to my parked vehicle. The heat wafting up from the parking lot made my spinning head want to fall off my neck. Bracing myself against my truck, I fumbled with the lock. After multiple tries, at last I gained entry. I flopped onto the driver's seat, knowing I should call somebody.

But I didn't.

I eased out of the parking space, sweating profusely, either from the copious amounts of courage I had consumed or the fear of subconsciously knowing I was already in way over my head. I left town, taking the back roads, hoping to avoid any trouble. It took all the concentration I had just to stay on the road. The pavement in front of me danced like a 12-foot piece of PVC pipe held at arm's length. I couldn't tell if the curves I saw coming before me were real or just imagined. While trying to observe a stop sign, I realized I had come to a halt on the far side of the intersection. Fortunately, no cross-traffic got in the way, so I stubbornly continued on.

A few minutes later, I nearly killed three people.

About four miles from home, a minivan driven by a woman with two children, probably on their way to school, topped a hill to find my pickup truck meeting them head on in the wrong lane.

It's amazing I even remember the details, but I can tell you, they're sharper in my memory to this day than just about anything in my checkered past.

I will *never* forget their faces in the windshield, silently screaming in horror.

I sluggishly braced for impact, throwing some sloppy subconscious correction into the steering wheel. With our combined closing speed of more than one-hundred miles an hour, the van whizzed by me in a blur, hitting the ditch and disappearing into a cloud of dust.

"Oh God!" I panicked.

Scenes of the TV news reports flashed around the outskirts of my scrambled brain.

I managed to bring my vehicle to a stop, fearing the worst, knowing I couldn't walk back to the scene of the crash without falling down.

Squinting into the rearview mirror, trying to keep myself still, I saw the dust settle to reveal the van, still upright and turned around 180 degrees.

It began moving, then pulled back onto the road, to my relief. My horror was now replaced with the alternative. The driver rolled down the window, shook her fist, and screamed something at me that I couldn't hear.

She turned the van around in the original direction she was headed, opened the door, stepped out, and headed toward me.

I had wound up on the wrong side of the road at the edge of a hill. I needed to get out of the way before someone crested it and t-boned me.

Assuming everybody in the van was okay, my senses dulled. I eased across the road to the other side and weaved my way home.

I have no recollection of passing any other traffic. If there weren't any, that was good; besides the squirming road in my impaired vision, the effects of an adrenaline crash pulled me toward passing out.

I fought the elephant, weaving back and forth across the road, winding my way down the home stretch. I remember feeling a flood of relief as I arrived at the turn into my driveway. I felt that false sense of accomplishment from actually beating the odds once again, and I congratulated myself at being slick enough to turn on my blinker for the left turn.

Then, I remember coming to, still in the road, my foot on the break, with the *tick- tick-tick* of the turn signal luring me back to semi-consciousness.

I turned in, crept up the driveway, and parked in front of the garage—miraculously without hitting it. With relief washing over me once more, I passed out again.

This time, I didn't come around until mid-day—the engine still idling.

My wife, Karen, wouldn't be home for several more hours. I gathered myself enough to get out of the truck and crawl upstairs, hoping to take a shower and begin to straighten up. I lay down across the bed for a moment.

The room spun wildly.

My heart thumped like a howitzer, and my head was being torn open with each pulse. I placed my hand over my eyes. It felt so bad; I thought I was going past puke mode straight toward a stroke.

I don't know how long I lay there, drifting in and out.

Much later in the day, as I transitioned from wasted to the beginnings of a vicious hangover, I guiltily relived the events of the morning.

I suddenly heard, *"That was your last chance!"* booming through the room.

I rose up, thinking a police officer or someone had followed me home and come into the house. It was very, very real, and very loud.

"I have spared you for the last time. You are on your own now. Do something about it."

"What? Who's there?" The gathering darkness moved my imagination to run wild. I felt a tremendous, powerful presence floating above me, as if it were looking right through me into the deepest reaches of my soul. It was powerful, but somehow caring, almost begging me to take heed of the warning. Whatever it was, I felt it knew me better than I wanted to know myself.

And it was tired of me not living right.

Instantly humbled and ashamed, I sat on the edge of the bed, reeling, but now very much awake. No one was there physically, of course, but I knew what I had heard.

I stared out the window into the gathering dusk where a whole day had passed—a day I had wasted.

Overwhelmed, and strangely filled with resolve, I said aloud, "I will. I will! I will try with all my heart," I spoke to whomever, whatever, or wherever that deep, authoritative-yet-compassionate voice came from.

I believe God loves us all unconditionally. It's hard to accept for me sometimes, but He does. I also believe in the saying, *"He helps those who help themselves."*

Thus began the time when I started to really help myself.

Karen, who of all things worked as a law enforcement officer for the U.S. Park Service at the time, came home late from work that night. I had finally fallen into a sleep that would carry me to the next morning.

Over coffee, and still suffering, I recounted to her what had happened. "I will be clean and sober for the rest of my days," I vowed, but I don't think she believed me. She had heard it so many times before while I ached through the agony of remorse-filled hangovers.

I had wanted to quit for many years. I always knew deep down, life would be better; but until now, I didn't believe it possible or important enough to tackle. I thought it could always wait till later.

This time was different. I had a lot more clarity and conviction, now that I had been scared straight. I had made a promise I very much feared to break.

At first it was easy, with the events of that day still haunting me. As time began to dull my reasons, sobriety got harder.

Going back on the road proved downright frightening. I was pretty much known as a party animal and a hellraiser for many years amongst my friends and enemies all. I had known some in the past who changed their lifestyles, and it always bred mistrust toward them on my part.

I couldn't stand it if anybody tried to preach to me. Stupid. Looking back, it was probably disguised envy. I should have admired them; I should have taken notes, instead.

I didn't proclaim anything to anybody. I just quietly withdrew from the party scene. To combat the after-show wild-side demons, I would retire to the bus and throw myself into studying for the Airline Transport Pilot written test that I was hoping to pass at the end of the Farewell Tour.

After passing up a lot of good times, most of the guys figured things out—understood that I had a struggle going on—and they gave me space without treating me any differently.

I remember after a few weeks into my goal, some of the guys jokingly said, "We can finally get some rest around here without the old Herndon on board!" It was their way of showing encouragement.

The triggers were hell at first, but I stubbornly refused to give in—mainly because I had begun to learn the beauty of performing straight. Every show, every after-show party I didn't give in to was like money in the bank for me.

I started to think of it like that. Each day became a deposit in my life account. I figured the penalties for early withdrawal were severe. I also didn't want to have to start all over again.

At home it proved just as difficult, if not more so. I always enjoyed happy hour in the evenings before dinner. Of course, happy hour would always turn into happy night, which created a special set of problems all its own. Surrounded by the comforts and security of home, I could easily slip. I had to fight really hard here.

I joined the North Lookout Mountain Volunteer Fire Department in Mentone, where we lived. While there, I worked quite a few motor vehicle accidents where driver impairment was the cause. The scenes reminded me of how close I came myself that watermark day, almost recklessly causing the very same horrible tragedy that would unfold before me as I worked those wrecks. It was terrifying. It cemented my will, and the reasons, to become sober.

I started drinking Diet 7-Up when I wanted to have just a couple. I love it to this day. I made myself believe the tickle of the carbonated beverage going down my pipe was the same as a cold beer. I willed myself to believe it and the triggers didn't pull at me so bad.

I began to realize, they all pass, and there is peace and *victory* on the other side. Some lasted a few minutes, some lasted hours—or days. The more I toughed it out, the easier it got with time.

Curious, I went to an AA meeting one night in Chattanooga. I just wanted to hear how others deal with a major life change. I came out a changed man. I heard spellbinding stories of unfathomable tragedy from people just like me, but who sadly were not nearly as lucky. I saw the path I had been headed down for years before I'd mercifully been turned away from it. It was another epiphany. I attended about a dozen more meetings, gaining resolve to accomplish my goal, and becoming confident in my new skin.

I am keenly aware that my experience with this is relatively minor compared to some, but that doesn't matter. Dedicating one's self to a life change-of-habit is daunting, no matter how high or low your bottom is. At this writing, I'm approaching my 12-year anniversary of the day that changed everything for the better immeasurably.

I know in my heart of hearts, I would not be here to tap the keyboard to write my story, if I had not heeded the stern warning I got from God above, my guardian angel, my conscience, or the combination of all three. A gift . . . for sure.

Looking back, I am so thankful for the gift. I am still scared straight and can say this is an instance where I feel it is comfortably safe to use the word "never."

CHAPTER 30

Sentence to Penance

When you eat, sleep, and live your starry-eyed dreams—as I did in the early days—you don't wonder if things might not be as good as they seem. Lust has no second thoughts.

Late one night in 1978, still living in Florence, South Carolina, I stopped at McDonald's for a midnight snack. The drive-thru was not yet a modern convenience, so I had to go to the counter to order my Big Mac.

The girl at the register, along with the help in the back, were all a-tither; they were all excited to see a gleaming tour bus pull into the parking lot. The 1970s pop group England Dan & John Ford Coley had played a show at Francis Marion College a few hours earlier, and were also making a stop for some late-night grub.

I got my burger and went out to take a look at this house on wheels. Hoping to get a glimpse inside, I stood there peering, but to no avail.

The road manager finally came out and went inside to place the band's food order. He looked a bit flustered, so I decided not to bug him. I grew tired of standing around, just gawking, so I headed to my car.

I remember thinking, *How cool is that? How fun it must be to play music to an adoring crowd, then jump on the bus like one big happy family and ride off into the night. How great that must be to head down the highway with every mile bringing you closer to doing what you love night after night. Ah! The camaraderie of hanging out with friends, having a few drinks, playing cards, watching movies or, writing the next hit song—all while riding in style. Wow!* To say I had a lot to learn is a classic understatement.

Tour busses sure enough are impressive. They're power on wheels, possessing the mythical glamour of showbiz. As for the glamour, well, that usually stops at the door. Inside the luxuriously appointed coaches, for the most part, you'll find some very tired and sometimes irritable folks who, after more than 330 days cooped up together under lots of stress, tend to get on one another's very last nerve.

After about our third consecutive year of non-stop touring, such was the case for me—one night in 1984. All that I had imagined, from seeing that tour bus at McDonald's, went right out the window when I found myself a tired, irritable man . . . and on *my* very last nerve.

The climate control onboard our bus became quite a matter of contention. A good night's sleep is hard enough to come by on the road, and when it's *hot* in the bunk, it's impossible.

For whatever reason, one of our singers didn't like air conditioning; he said the cool air dried out his throat, and that interfered with his vocal performance. Since he had the clout, he set the thermostat to his liking while the rest of us sweated it out. It was so uncomfortable that another player started flying commercially to avoid the sauna ride.

I couldn't afford the airline tickets, and the other band member was caught between a rock and a hard place trying to keep the peace. The remaining onboard staff had no say so whatsoever. There would be no compromise. The logic from the singer, and eventually management, was that if the singer lost his voice, there would be no shows and thus no income. It may have seemed logical, but it was entirely arbitrary on the singer's part.

Those of us who couldn't get any rest became very fatigued; some got sick from being so run down.

This didn't seem fair to me or to others who, though maybe not as important as the core members, had worked just as hard to contribute in their respective roles.

Morale began to tank, but people seemed reluctant to speak up and address the issue. In the grand scheme of things, it seemed to me that we were all walking on eggshells about a rather trivial matter.

We were going to play the University of Notre Dame arena. Unusually for our fast, breakneck pace, we had arrived the evening before. Parked in the lot of our hotel, I was looking forward to a good night's sleep in a real bed, being able to breathe the cool air of a hotel room.

I got out of my bunk, sweating from the heat, and ready to check into my room. The others were milling about, gathering their things to take off the bus. I reckon I had reached my limit of tolerance, because I felt foolishly inclined to speak on others' behalf. For whatever the reason, I did.

I don't recall exactly what I said, but it was something to the effect of, "I'm glad you can get all the beauty sleep you need inside this furnace, but there's six or seven others on here who can't. It ain't all about you!"

After blinking in surprise, he replied, saying something that threw me into a rage that charted my course for the remainder of my years with the band.

I came out of my seat—lunging toward him—ready to have it out. Catching me in mid-air, six-foot-four badass—ex-steel worker and ex-bouncer from the Bowery—Bruce Burnett grabbed me midflight, and put me into a sleeper hold. It took the fight right out of me.

I vaguely remember lying on the floor, floating around the edge of unconsciousness, looking up at Bruce. He asked, "Are you done now, bud?"

I had seen Bruce in action as a bouncer many nights in Myrtle Beach. Despite his gruff, frank demeanor, I always liked him. Bruce always seemed like a tough senior NCO—non-commissioned officer—in a military outfit to me. He held a commanding presence, and we pretty much did what he said. We all had a healthy respect for him. I know I was always reluctant to cross him.

After I got up and got my bearings, I got my room key and went to the hotel without anything further said. The band member I'd lunged toward was nowhere in sight. I went to the bar for a nightcap where a couple of other guys from the bus sat on their bar stools, avoiding me like the plague.

I awoke late the next day with regrets about losing my cool. I tempered it, thinking, *Well, this is a band. Bands are like family and all families fight once in a while. I reckon I can just go apologize to the guy, say I didn't feel good or whatever, and we can move on. Who knows, maybe we might start some convo to reach a compromise on the thermostat.* It didn't turn out that way. Not in the least.

Right before sound check, I was summoned to a vacant dressing room back-stage by Dale Morris, the band's manager. The ass-chewing I anticipated never came. Instead, I got a sentence for my crime. He gave me a chance to explain my actions; he listened, but didn't comment. He sat there, shaking his head.

Quiet for a moment, he began with an icy stare, then followed with, "Mark, until it's formally decided whether or not to dismiss you from the group, you are to have no contact, in any way whatsoever, with any of the three principal members. You are not to speak to, get near to, or participate with them in any activities other than your performance on stage. I have someone who can come and take your place tonight if need be." He paused long enough for me to take a breath. "However, they wish to wait and do a few shows before any major changes are made. Do not attempt to contact any one of them regarding this matter. As for transportation, you will ride on the crew bus from now on. If we have to fly, you will either be ticketed on another flight or be seated in another part of the aircraft away from where the principals are seated. Do I make myself clear?"

He made himself clear.

He left me in the dressing room, alone with my thoughts. I was mad at first—not at him; he was just the messenger—but because I thought the whole thing was spinning out of control. I thought this was something that could have been resolved long before I showed my ass.

Being so shortsighted at the time, I replaced my anger with musings about all the fun I would have on the crew bus with my fellow hellraisers during my numbered days. Such is the impetuousness of youth.

Over the years, I paid dearly for this—financially, as well as mentally and physically. In retrospect, I probably should have kept my mouth shut.

One reason began to feed another in a dangerous spiral of self-righteousness, denial, and self-destruction, which led me down some trails that I will always regret. Then again, it wasn't *all* bad. Despite my exile, I had some glorious times and, even now, I wouldn't trade the memories for anything.

Obviously, I never lost my gig. I did gradually assume the mantle of the black sheep in the band and, of course, I tried to prove I deserved it whenever I could. Hindsight shows me how stupid that was. I missed out on a lot—the songwriting, for example. I missed out on some of the contributions I could have made to the band's creative process and evolution over the decades.

Eventually, to the surprise of all our fans and especially me, I would be told that all those decades I was never even in the band. I will never think I deserved that, but I take responsibility for my actions. I'm sure I missed out on a lot of things, but that's the way it went down.

A footnote...

One night in the late '90s, I was actually on board the band bus, hitching a ride home from an event in Nashville. Fifteen years and a million miles had passed beneath wings and wheels since that fateful night at Notre Dame. Old bygones had long since faded, and there really was no animosity in the air.

I still rode the crew bus to gigs, but it was by my choice at this point, mainly because the band traveled by day and the crew traveled by night. I liked riding the bus through the night.

Randy and Teddy had gone to their bunks to catch a nap. I was up talking with the driver and our media-relations guy; we got to laughing about our road manager, who was Steve Boland at the time. Steve had a habit of waking up violently from his bunk when disturbed. He apparently experienced frequent nightmares.

Just like Bruce, Steve was not to be trifled with. He was built like a bull, and just as strong.

A little of my old mischievous self crept back in momentarily, and I decided to go mess with him. I went back and opened his curtain ever so slowly.

The two up front, who giggled along with me, kept saying, "Don't do it, man. Don't do it! You'll be sorry!" I've never acquiesced to "don't" or "can't;" so that only egged me on.

I began laying French fries on his beard, then said in a whisper, "Steve, you're missing catering, man. Wake up; the food is great!"

Coming around, he struck out at me with all his might, intending a death punch. I went flying across the aisleway—envision a horse kicking a squirrel—and right into the bunk with Teddy, who also awoke, unhappy. Not knowing what had happened, he shoved me out of his bunk, cussing appropriately.

I was laughing, nearly in hysterics, when Randy awoke and snatched his bunk curtain open. I was sitting on the aisle floor trying to regain my composure while the other guys up front became mum.

Randy rolled his head out of the bunk and with great pause for effect, sighed and said, "Now I remember why we threw his ass off here in the first place!"

We all, including Steve and Teddy, busted out laughing. During those short hours, it felt like old times when things were good . . . before the storm of success changed personalities and perspectives.

CHAPTER 31

Building Bridges

A promoter presented the concept of the American Farewell Tour (AFT) to the four of us in a meeting in the fall of 2002. I was invited to attend. This struck me as a little odd, given that I'd never participated in the monthly business meetings in the past. Only the three band principals and their business manager attended.

I was flattered in a way; it made me feel included in the planning stages of what was shaping up to be the biggest tour of the band's career. The details of the meeting have long since faded, but I recall the vision that the promoter and management held for the project. I was excited.

At last, we were going to *look* big time. All of the details in putting on a first-rate, professional road show were being addressed—from having a really cool access laminate, to providing a classy hospitality suite. Prior to now, we just never had the time to place a concentrated focus on all the details. A budget was established for a state-of-the-art production, giving the fans something they could be proud of. *Their* band would look and sound world-class—not that we were slack by any means before; it was just going to be *so* much better.

Since the beginning days of my love affair with concert performances, I've always paid attention to the production side of stagecraft. In addition to the actual live musical delivery, I've always been interested in how things work—lighting, rigging, sound, stage layout, etc.

With this in mind, soon after our planning meeting, I volunteered to be the liaison responsible for various elements in creating the fresh new look for the AFT.

Previously, I had spent a lot of my off time flying OH-58 helicopters all over the state with the Alabama State Troopers. I flew in support of the marijuana eradication program carried out annually every summer.

As part of the long nine- and ten-hour daily missions, I began to notice a common element: steel girder bridges, both railroad and automotive, spanned nearly ever river and stream across the landscape. They were throwbacks to another time in history, a time before the interstates came.

We flew low and, in some cases, even *under* those bridges. Getting a good look at how the structures were built, I began to form the idea to model one of these trestle-type designs as a backdrop for the stage. I wanted to show how our

20 some-odd years of touring had bridged the gap between musical styles and stereotypes. I wanted that bridge to convey the bond I felt we had established among devoted fans from all walks of life and every generation. I wanted them to know we recognized our part in bridging that gap and, like them, we were just four ordinary folks who shared something unique.

With the help of the design company, we managed to pull it off.

From a house perspective, it was really cool. When the show started, the giant bridge model lay in a heap of what looked like random metal beams. As the show progressed, very slowly, almost imperceptibly, the heap moved gradually to reveal two halves of a steel bridge rising. It resembled a drawbridge moving in reverse.

The show ran more than three hours; the bridge assembly mysteriously formed. The lighting and video effects deterred the audience from consciously detecting the set evolution.

Ultimately, the two halves were joined to form a complete span across the stage. The bridge connected the eastern and western halves of America, displayed on two massive backdrops framing the whole scene. It was very effective, and I was proud of my part in making it a reality.

During the development of the concept and stage build, I began to think that this tour was going to be my last chance to better myself financially. I felt like my personal contributions to the success of the band were significant, and it had been a long time since I had seen any increase in my compensation. I had never made any demands, never missed a show, and always gave my all. My years of loyalty, my contributions toward introducing a new kind of country to rock audiences— I felt I deserved some recognition with a better take-home from all this, from our last hurrah . . . our last go-round.

So, I carefully prepared my idea and presented my proposal.

A meeting was held, and my contract with the business entity that constituted the band was finally renegotiated.

I was filled with hopeful anticipation.

I envisioned all the ways this would help my family and me.

For the first time in my life, I expected long overdue financial security; and for the first time in my career I expected some acknowledgement for my role in making this band bigger than what any of us could do alone.

CHAPTER 32

Slipping Beneath the Waves

It hurts to set you free
But you'll never follow me
The end of laughter and soft lies
The end of nights we tried to die

This is the end

"The End" The Doors

*   *   *

Bismarck, ND—October 18, 2004 . . . The Last Show

I couldn't miss the irony. The *Bismarck* was a WWII state-of-the-art German battleship sunk in the North Atlantic after skeptics said she couldn't be beaten.

Here we were, going down for the last time in a town with the same name. Nothing against this fine city, of course. People of German descent, immigrating to this part of the country, would name their town after Otto von Bismarck, the first chancellor of the German Empire in the mid-1800s. Nonetheless, the semantics with the battleship name and its fate seemed appropriate for the way I felt that night.

The fall chill seemed to permeate everything—my jacket, the arena, even on board the buses parked outside. It crept in like a harbinger of the long, severe winter waiting to lock this part of the world in its vice-like jaws.

A shiver ran up my spine. That harbinger might be a premonition of the cold uncertainty of what lay ahead—after we would pack up the trucks later that night for the last time.

This would be the last show ever; I was about to face a drastic change in lifestyle coming at me as fast as an Alberta Clipper. My whole way of life was about to end.

After the last song, at the close of the show, people who had worked, sweated, bled, cried, and laughed together for a quarter-century would head separate ways. It didn't seem real. It didn't seem enough of an epitaph for such an entity that had been through so much.

I, for one, thought we should have held that final show in perhaps a more poignant, more historically significant setting, since this was *the end*—not only for the band, but also for the fans. Perhaps a special event in our hometown of Ft. Payne—or Myrtle Beach, where it all started—would have been a good closer.

People were tired and burned out from years and years on the road. The atmosphere was festive with a free-at-last energy, right?

Wrong.

The finality was oppressive after the show. We came off stage, leaving behind fans crying openly. We found no party atmosphere—no celebration backstage. A few purely functionary toasts and well wishes where exchanged amongst friends and colleagues, and that was it.

Twenty-eight years of doing what we all did, and surviving despite it, came to an unceremonious screeching halt. After the backstage area had cleared except for the cleanup crews, I wandered into one of the vacant dressing rooms deep inside the arena. I found a metal chair, so I sat, alone and numb; the steady dripping of water in the shower accented the stillness.

I didn't want to leave.

I never wanted to leave this spot. If I did, it would be confronting the very reality I was trying to hide from.

At last, I forced myself to walk out into the arena. I picked out a seat in the bleachers and sat watching the load-out activities below. It never dawned on me some twenty years prior, happily reflecting in a seat in the Carolina Coliseum, that I would do the same thing again in this place, but with a feeling of complete emptiness.

As the road cases were pushed off toward the waiting trucks, the light trusses in their set carts rolled down the ramps, and the last pieces of rigging were lowered out of the steel above, nagging questions whirled in my head:

Will anybody remember?

I felt as though a part of me stayed on that loading dock—watching the buses and trucks cast off to disappear into the dark prairie night that closed over it all like a heavy stage curtain.

Feeling empty, I stepped onto the bus and out of a life. I sat and stared at the town silently through the window and wondered: Will all of this fade into irrelevance? What was it all for?

The answers to those questions, coming with hindsight and some perspective now are . . .

Yes, people will remember, but not as many as you think.

Yes, everything does fade into irrelevance.

What it was all for, well, it was for a while.

Recalling that night makes me very sad. There was no closure, only a disconnected, dysfunctional final scene. I felt like I was in a movie theatre, dumbstruck after an epic film, watching the credits roll. However, no screen loomed in front of me, just the all-too-familiar sounds and sights of load-out echoing off the walls and rafters.

Surrounded by thousands of empty post-partum seats, I sat alone in that venue watching a great ship slipping quietly beneath the coming waves of time.

A Parting Word

After a successful tour, with arenas jam-packed and thousands of bodies in seats, the promise of financial security for me was never met.

It never happened, and that was that.

Well, not entirely just *that*.

What happened next is a matter of public record, and for me, a matter of private pain. It was the greatest disappointment of my life.

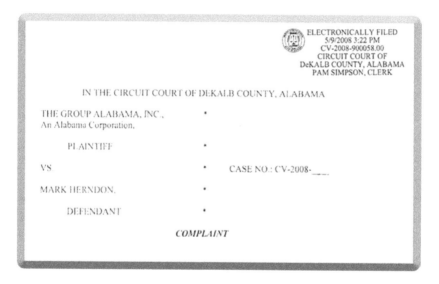

My contributions to the band, the shows, the fans—I'll leave that to the music-business historians to decide if I mattered. I think I know what the fans think. They're still telling me.

I didn't include any of the hundreds of accolades the band received over the years because that's already been done. Award shows, and the glitz and glamour stuff, while sometimes fun, always made me feel like a fish out of water. The fleeting glory was nice, but I never felt all that special because of it—just lucky. I was never in it for the recognition; I was in it for the music, and to connect with people.

Of course, I celebrated plenty back then; it did feel good to be part of a group so acclaimed. Still, that would usually pass the next day or two—along with the hangover.

Later, with somewhat of a clearer head and the hubris fading, I would think about how much more we owed the fans for being recognized with such prestigious accolades. To me, a band should go out there and prove *why* they are cleaning house every year at the big award shows.

I always wanted to improve our performances, regardless of how state-of-the-art our production was. I wanted us to look worthy of the praise, musically, theatrically, and relevantly. Maybe we did, but I was never satisfied. To me, the sword can never be sharp enough. Being on top, as they say, carries a lot of responsibility and obligation to your craft.

Maybe not making the money most people think someone in my position would have is another blessing. I am able to enjoy the simple life a lot easier now because of it. If my role would have been more lucrative back then, it might have killed me. From what I've observed over the years, sudden wealth is a curse on most who receive it. It's abnormal. Innocent dreams and passions are exploited more obscenely in the entertainment business than anywhere. You pay the piper one way or another, and it's a hell of an expense for your soul.

The biggest part of me paid the piper for so many years because I loved the life. If I'm a fool for doing that, then so be it. Fools can sometimes be wealthier than the rich.

I didn't write this book to sling anything, to say anything bad about anyone. The dirt has been shared time and time again in other books, about other bands. It all sounds the same after a while.

No, this book is simply about who I was, how I got to live my dreams and even realize new ones. I wanted to share the stories that enriched my life in one way or another. I hoped to share the human side of the often mystique-shrouded road life. Maybe I lifted the veil a little.

The thing I treasure the most is a taste of success in a field I loved. I will always miss the traveling, the flying, the concerts, the fans, and the friendships I made along the way. Some would doubt this, but I absorbed a lot about life on that fast-paced highway. For every story you have just read, there are many more like it. Perhaps I will get to some of those another time.

I don't know if there will ever again be a group that enjoys such a long run. I doubt the power brokers in the music business today would allow it. I wonder if consumers today would support it.

When I think of those nearly thirty years we spent crisscrossing this continent, it all seems unbelievable. But, 1) it *really* happened and 2) it's *really* over.

Those were heady times. Although it doesn't bother me, I have come to know the cold shoulder of a business that used to welcome me with open arms and now yawns in my face. In some circles, I am what you call a has been.

I used to wonder about that when we would sweep the award shows in the heydays. I would watch the old timers (back then) and wonder how they felt watching us. Were they being shown to the door in the cruel way this business so callously hands out its terms of appreciation? Did they resent us? Were they bitter from the patronizing that comes with faded glory? I don't know. Most all were professionals. I especially remember Tammy Wynette, who was always so wonderfully gracious whenever we crossed paths.

Even though we *all* worked very hard for them, I always managed to feel a little out of place being handed those trophies by someone whose own spotlights were beginning to dim. "Spoils to the victor," they say, but it was humbling for me.

While typing this manuscript way into the wee hours, sometimes I would take a break and go outside. Memories of landscapes and cityscapes filling the bus windows, sliding beneath airplane wings . . . days and nights in far off places from times long gone . . . these would replay on a screen just behind my eyes. I recalled towns I came to know almost as well as my home. I relived random moments I hadn't thought about in years.

Faces flickered in the blackness.

Stars above looked like cigarette lighters held high at a concert.

The colors of spotlight beams, thick with smoke and energy, spearing down through the darkness from high perches—they played off arena walls rising from the perimeter of my yard.

I felt the old thrill in my gut again. I would stand behind the stage curtain, waiting to leap up on the drum riser, energized to feel the power of the crowd and to hear the reverberations of guitar and drums echoing about the lofty room. I would be peering out my hotel room window at the sea of people crowding the streets and sidewalks, hurrying to be the first to enter the stadium just a few blocks away—just like me years earlier.

Standing outside my front door, I shook my head with the realization of the very bigness of this thing, and what we did, how it really was, and how hard it had been to get there. Then I recalled the reason *why* we did it from the beginning.

From somewhere beyond the tree line of my yard, the sound of thousands, cheering from the floor to the nosebleed section, resounded in my ears to pull me through the fog of old memory into lucidity. Sitting there on my front porch steps, I was immersed in palpable moments from the past in vivid detail: great nights on stage, moments in places that would later go into the history books, living the dream again . . . and basking in it.

The images danced in my head with such clarity that I felt as though I was a time traveler, transported back to see it all happen again in real time.

With a million words gathering in my heart and brain, I would rush back to the keyboard. These words would pour out like people trying to escape a fire in a packed building; I couldn't get them all out in time, and some perished in the mental bonfire.

I hope I at least rescued some of them in time to share with you. I hope, too, that some of these look-backs were interesting, funny, and maybe even at least a little bit poignant.

I realize some people have stories that make mine seem very small, such as my old next-door neighbor in Mentone, Richard Fergusson, who found himself high over Nazi Germany in 1943 with his guts shot out and lying in his lap. He struggled to pilot a damaged four-engine bomber back to England. Fergusson had the presence of mind to stuff his organs back into his body and pour water from his canteen over the horrid wound. In that high altitude, the water froze, thus cauterizing the bleeding. He managed to make it back to his home field, saving the lives of his crew. To my knowledge he never got any medals, nor did he seek any. He would say, "I was just doin' my job. Hell, I lived to come home, and many didn't."

Stories like these are stories of *true* hardship, loss, survival and great perseverance. I've heard some of these from everyday folks I met on the road over the years. They are stunning in comparison to mine. Nonetheless, I felt compelled to write this book.

Thanks for listening. May you, too, seize a chance to live your dreams.

Acknowledgements

"Living the dream," as the saying goes, is not possible without others. I would like to thank some of them for helping make living my dream a reality:

First, to the **Good Lord Above**, for answering my prayers so long ago, and to my **guardian angel**, whoever he or she is. I have been very, very blessed. I still wonder why.

My parents (RIP): Thank you for always showing me, by example, how to keep my eyes wide open and my head up. I miss you both very much.

My daughter, Katie: I thank God again and again that you came to this Earth as my daughter. Through you, I realized a much higher circle of living as a father. You are extraordinary, my precious soulmate kid.

My former wife, Karen: The good times were great. There never could have been a better mother for our daughter.

To many of my friends on **the crew** and **"hired guns"** for many years: **Hampton** *"Scuba"* Osborne (RIP), Joe *"Dixie"* Fuller, Ed *"Five minutes!"* Turner, Danny *"The Hoser"* Love, Bob *"Beaulah!"* Martin, Bob House (RIP), Dave *"Hud"* Haney, Joe *"I'm Roadieone"* Carpenter, Bruce *"Wildweed"* Burnett, Jeff *"Have a good rock show!"* Rucks, Mike *"Moses"* Beck, Joe *"Too-Tall"* Stogner, David *"Muffy"* Zammit, Bill *"Ott"* Mimbs (RIP) *"Johnnymac"* Kuy-kendall, Richey, Dino *"O-Nid"* Pastin, Dave Haskell, Larry *"The Condor!"* Hanson, Paul *"Paulie"* Binkley, Chris *"Nick Danger"* Walters, Del *"Papa"* Rucks, Phillybob, Joey *"Driver"* Thrasher (RIP). In the beginning our escapades were big and oh, so much fun. I could not have made it through the later, harder, dystopian years if I had not been a part of that unique brotherhood. I especially thank a few more:

Mike *"Go Monkey"* Neeley: We fought the law and the law lost. My final logbook entry from that era reads: "Wright Bros Monument low altitude pass. Vne plus 20. Farewell faithful bird". I can only imagine what you wrote in yours. You never got the creds you deserved. Cat 2 in Portland, a circling approach in Amarillo, a trap at Miramar, and a divert to Catalina. Ha! Blue skies and tailwinds, Cap'n.

Charlie Daniels: You changed the outcome for me with profound advice on fans. You were right; the return lasts a lifetime.

Todd "*Mater*" Hale: Nothing says "We're in the big time now!" like a hundred miles of freezing our asses off in a broken car chained to the back of a rusty roll-top tow truck. Thanks for all the laughs, old pal.

Brent "*Spot*" Barrett: You should teach a university course on people skills. The good reputation we enjoyed with venues and promoters came largely in part from what you did for us every day.

Rick "*Hand*" Dickson: Glad you took the wheel when you did. I hope you never catch another "fish" like that one in Snake River Canyon. Semper Fi.

Gary "*Bigun*" Freeman: You defined "true blue" out there, bro. Steadfast. By the way, "Lil Buddy" got his foot back.

Kevin O'Keefe, Esq.: The devil's in the details, but he forgot one, didn't he? Thanks for the diligence.

John "*Bigdog*" Clark: A "borrowed" chopper, a detour at Tuskegee, and hearing the radials come to life again. Cleared hot, weapons free. I got your six, my friend.

Phil McClendon: Great pilot, friend. I owe you many thanks for help up the aviation ladder when I needed it. "Hey, can we stay *one* more hour in the sim?"

The countless ATC controllers all over the U.S. who got to know us at the other end of a radio beam. They helped us meet a sometimes-impossible schedule in more ways than anyone can ever know.

Eric Paiste: Your company makes the finest cymbals on the planet. Thanks to you and **Rich Mangicero** for always treating me like an artist *despite* my abilities.

To the many unsung people on our home staff who performed thankless tasks: **The Fan Club** employees, especially **Karen Potts, Jeneane Hamby,** and **Kim Armstrong,** who devotedly managed the tons of mail and PR; **the riggers,** who spent long days suspended hundreds of feet up in the rafters of arenas and barns to hang the show; **the drivers** and **wire guys; the light dogs** and **sound guys.** I didn't get to know some of you, but I appreciate the hard-ass work you did for us.

Gaynelle Pitts: Great job pulling off the impossible every June for sixteen years straight. I don't know how you did it. You left before I could ever say thanks, so here it is.

Randy, Teddy, and Jeff: To three members of the hardest-working four-man band that ever was. We brought great music to the world, and the world brought us our dreams. None of us would ever have realized those dreams without all of us. In my own way, I admire the part you played.

The Fans: A million thanks to a million of you. I hope I gave back at least some of what you so beautifully gave to me. You helped us create something bigger than any of us could alone, and it belonged to you. You bought the records. You came to the shows. You bought me a ticket to live the fantasy, moments in the spotlight at my Theater of Realized Dreams. Until I depart the fix outbound, I will always yearn to do it again somehow, in some other way, perhaps in another life. To be part of something big. Like a falling star, I will either burn up on reentry, or actually land somewhere trying. I can't sit still. The show goes on, and it's showtime somewhere. I'm not through yet. Till then, and even though someday it may be in a chair, I'll be ready to rock.

This book could not have been possible without the guidance of the following people:

Jamie Bowman: I never would have picked up a stick again if not for those loud Saturday nights in the "Hell House" . . . *Freebird!*

Leah Seawright: Best friend, soulmate, and road warrior—the greatest natural talent I have ever performed with. I never thought I would feel it again, but you brought joy back to the stage. Thank you for pushing me when I most needed it during this project. Your story of survival is a mindbender. Write that book. It will be awesome.

Mark Estes, Jamie Bell, Nathan Hiett, Chris Patterson, Kevin Jenne, Johnny Adams, Stevo Johnson, Chopper Wilson, Truman Virden, Terry Parker, Kevin Hyler, Tracy Walker—*Great* musicians all. Been gigging and recording with these guys since the Farewell Tour. Many shows, many new stories . . . some might even make another book.

To everybody who encouraged me to realize this book project, including **Sharon May,** who proofed drafts and helped in many ways, and **Desiree Scott,** author, who introduced me to the world of publishing.

Noel "The Bald" Webster: You were always on my side. Thanks for the skinny on the copyright matrix.

Kat Atwood: I knew I had come to the right place when I met you and your staff at **Music City Media**. Your diligence, polish, and patience is exactly what this project and I needed for a successful book launch and more.

Jason Perkins: I dumped a rough concept on the table at **Jason Perkins Designs** and you got it immediately. Thanks for the coolest cover artwork, and for speaking your mind when you did.

Ann Stewart, my book designer at **Fresh Ink Group:** You excelled at pulling together all the files for print layouts and digital formatting in record-breaking time.

Stephen Geez, my editor and publisher at **Fresh Ink Group:** Stephen, you and **Beem Weeks** and the rest of your team earned my trust even as you worked hard to help me realize another dream. Thank you for your diligence and attention to detail.

CEEYA!

Mark Herndon

Legendary Country Music Hall of Fame drummer Mark Herndon yearned to fly jets as a military brat, then discovered the dream of playing drums, vowing to come back one day and perform at the very place where he once had to stand outside just to hear. Along the way, he loved and lost and made plenty of mistakes, persevering to achieve all that he imagined before having so much taken away. After decades with one of the most celebrated bands of all time, he still lives his dreams, playing, producing, flying, and now writing with keen observations about life and living in the spotlight.

Find Mark Herndon on Social Media

www.MarkHerndon.com

www.FreshInkGroup.com

Facebook: www.facebook.com/MarkHerndonFriendsandFans/?ref=hl

Twitter: @theMarkHerndon

Instagram: theMarkHerndon

The Fresh Ink Group

Publishing
Memberships
Share & Read Free Stories, Essays, Articles
Free-Story Newsletter
Writing Contests

Books
E-books
Amazon Bookstore

Authors
Editors
Artists
Professionals
Publishing Services
Publisher Resources

Members' Websites
Members' Blogs
Social Media

www.FreshInkGroup.com

Email: info@FreshInkGroup.com

Twitter: @FreshInkGroup

Google+: Fresh Ink Group

Facebook.com/FreshInkGroup

LinkedIn: Fresh Ink Group

About.me/FreshInkGroup

9 781936 442232